# Slipping Away

CW00926321

## One man's battle with Alzheimer's

Lynnette Lee

# Foreword

A couple of years ago, my sister and I noticed that something 'wasn't quite right' with dad. Nothing concrete, just little signs, and only every now and again. Dad was always a very strong character, full of life and laughter. Always cheerful and never had a bad word to say about anyone. Never one to take sides in an argument and he positively loved the fact that everyone was unique and should be treated accordingly.

Ever the optimist, he'd turn his hand to anything, and everything generally turned out well for him. His own father used to joke, "George, if you fell in the canal, you'd come out with a fish in your pocket!"

Teaching us all from a young age that if you believed in yourself enough and tried hard enough, anything and everything was possible. He told my sister and I that we could walk on water if we truly believed we could, which we found to be a slight untruth on his part when we next went swimming.

Dad loved nothing better than a good debate and would easily argue black was white, and white was then blue. His superpower was to argue so convincingly, the conversation would subtly be turned on its head, and before you knew it, he'd state your argument as his own.

He was good like that.

Born in 1935, he had one older and one younger sister. With his father away at the war, in essence dad took on the role of the man of the house, looking after the chickens, ducks and rabbits and providing eggs and meat for the table.

As a young teen he delivered fruit and vegetables for a local greengrocer, and his younger sister loved to ride on the flat basket on the front of his bike, up and down the street.

For as long as he can recall, he's always played the trumpet and throughout his life has played for many brass bands.

Joining the Army in 1955, he and my mam, Audrey met around the same time at Butlin's in Filey; him travelling from the Midlands and her coming from Sunderland. They maintained a long-distance romance for a while, then didn't see each other for a good few months until he hitchhiked up to marry her. The story goes that running out of money on their honeymoon, he brought her down to stay with his parents in Hinckley while he took on a casual bricklaying job for the week.

Mam was so laid back though; she would have taken all of this in her stride.

There was one story he loved to tell us about his first posting to Germany. There were no married quarters available, and mam was stuck in Sunderland. She complained to dad that she thought that married life meant they would be together, and he told her to write down exactly what he was about to say. He then drafted a letter that she sent to his commanding officer, threatening to leave him if the situation didn't change. Lo and behold, a house became available albeit 35 miles from camp. Dad commuted and filled up jerry cans with petrol to subsidise his travel costs, quickly gaining a reputation for being the 'King of the

Claims'. If there was an expense claim to be had, he was on it.

Whilst in Germany, the first four children came along, of which I'm the youngest.

In 1970 we all moved to England where dad was posted to Halifax, Bradford and then to Gillingham. I remember much of my childhood in Gillingham; long hot sunny days at the seaside, playing out 'until the streetlamps came on' and scrumping apples from the garden at the top of the alleyway. On Sunday dad would take me along to the Sergeant's Mess where he'd go for a lunchtime pint or two. He'd stand me on a barstool and my reward for singing 'Long haired lover from Liverpool' was a bag of mixed nuts. Happy times.

Mam and dad then realised their lifelong dream; moving out of Army Quarters and managing to buy their own house in Hinckley. Dad moved up first to renovate the house and us kids would excitedly call him from the phone box next to the park. I don't know which was most exciting, talking to dad or using an actual phone!

But not six months after we moved, disaster struck. Mam found a lump under her arm in the December, diagnosed as cancer. She died just four months later aged 43, leaving four devastated children ranging from 9 to 19 years old.

A few months later, whilst organising the Army bit of the Leicester Air Show, dad met his second wife, Pat. Soon, they were an item, and before long she moved into our house, bringing along her young daughter, a scrap of a thing, with a mop of unruly blonde hair who would become my sister and best friend. In due course they married, and shortly after, our little brother came along, making us a family of six children. When dad left the Army, he turned his hand to many occupations, including making concrete garden gnomes, being a postman and even an HGV lorry driving instructor at one point.

Eventually, he and Pat bought the house next door, knocked the two houses into one and ran a successful guest house for several years. Sadly, Pat also developed cancer and she succumbed to this terrible disease after a long, brave fight and died at home aged just 51. She left behind our youngest brother and sister aged just 14 and 19.

Never one to really enjoy his own company, Dad soon met Mary and they too were married. A couple of years back, Mary's health was suffering, so they took the difficult decision that she would go to live with her daughter, and dad would stay in their house. Still happily married, they would meet up for visits, walks and lunch regularly. It just happened that they lived in different houses as they had different needs.

Noticing the subtle but small changes, my sister and I put them down to senior moments. He'd tell you something and would tail off as though somebody had stolen the words. He'd put things down and not remember where they were. But, we reasoned, everyone did this when they were getting on a bit… didn't they?

If we broached the subject of his memory, he would vehemently deny anything was wrong, or that he was different in any way. He has always had a fear of the Doctor's, and I can probably count on one hand the number of times I know he's ever gone – so there was no chance of getting him in for an appointment willingly. It was time to go undercover, or sneaky beaky, whatever you might want to call it. My siblings and I all agreed that we needed a second opinion, it was just a matter of how we could get this.

I took matters into my own hands. Calling into his GP surgery I asked to have a quick word with his doctor. Voicing our dilemma about his deteriorating memory, his changes in behaviour, together with his reluctance to visit the doctor, his doctor came up with a cunning plan.

Knowing that dad had recently had some routine blood tests, he'd send him a letter to dad to call him in to talk about the results. I would bring him to the appointment, and while we were there, the Doctor would ask him some memory related questions.

Genius!

I duly collected him on the day of the appointment and off we went to see his doctor. The doctor began with the good news. Dad's blood test results were all OK, with nothing untoward showing up, which dad seemed happy about.

The doctor then chatted amiably about dad's health in general; how was he feeling? Dad replied that he felt healthy and well.

"And how's your memory? Do you find it difficult to remember things?"

Dad looked momentarily puzzled as he thought this one through.

After a slight pause and a nod, he replied slowly, "Yes."

"Can you tell me your address? Where do you live?"

Again, a pause whilst dad was turning this question over in his mind.

Laughing, he replied, "No! But I can tell you where it is! Out there, down the hill."

It was obvious that dad was recreating his route home in his head, but to say it was slightly worrying that he had no idea of the street or house number confirmed to me that we'd made the right decision to make the appointment.

The doctor continued, "While you are here, would you mind if we did a few tests to see how your memory is?"

I may have imagined this, but dad seemed to visibly relax. It was as though he knew there was something wrong, and now was his chance to find out exactly what.

He nodded his agreement.

"OK then. Who is the Prime Minister?"

Dad looked blank. This was concerning as he's always been a staunch Conservative. He was Margaret Thatcher's number one fan back in the day and had always been up for a good ~~discussion~~ argument around politics.

"No, I don't know" was the reply.

The doctor continued, "Not to worry" he said gently. "Let's try another one. How many animals can you name?"

Dad perked up a little bit. "Dog" he said, firmly. A slight pause, then "Cat". A furrow of his brow and a less confident "Horse".

After that no more animals came forth. He could only name three.

The doctor then asked him to draw a clock with the hands saying two o'clock.

Dad took pen to paper and drew a spidery circle for the clock face. He then drew a few dashes around the circumference which would signify the numbers. When it came to drawing the clock hands, he drew a few practice lines in the air, let his pen touch the paper then took it away again. I could tell that he couldn't understand how this simple task could be so difficult. How many times in his life must he have looked at a clock face? Eventually he dropped the pen on the paper, shook his head and said softly, "no."

As dad had failed all the questions dismally, this was officially the start of our journey with Alzheimer's.

Alzheimer's is an irreversible, progressive brain disorder that slowly destroys memory and thinking skills. Someone once described it to me like a very tall bookcase will all the books on it containing your memories. Your younger years are books on the bottom shelves, middle years are books in the middle and latter years at the very top. Imagine that the bookcase is unsteady and starts to rock from side to side. Books on the top shelves are the ones to slowly fall out first with the lower shelves taking longer to dislodge. This would explain why people can't often remember what they did yesterday but can vividly recall events from their childhood.

In the autumn of 2018, a brain scan confirmed the diagnosis and dad was referred on to the memory clinic.

This we would attend each month, with dad still unable to draw clocks or name animals, but much to the amusement of the memory nurse, demonstrated that his flirting skills were still on top form. After about six months the memory clinic signed dad back over to his GP as there was nothing further they could do for him. This is where I think dad fell through the cracks a little bit. Unless we made an appointment for something specific, nobody called him back to assess his memory. It felt like all the decisions were now up to us to make.

That was the first step in a long battle that's been hard work and frustrating in some parts, and hilarious in others. I'm never sure whether we laugh hysterically at things because they are genuinely funny, or because if we didn't laugh, we'd crack up.

Dad's not perfect, and this book doesn't set out to paint him as such. He's human, the same as everyone else. To see him gradually slip away from the strong, independent, forthright, (some might say bossy) man of the past, and grow more dependant, confused, sometimes frightened old man is heart-breaking, but I feel that his story deserves to be told.

In dad's back bedroom, there are numerous pairs of glasses of various ages, dubious conditions, and nobody really knows the strength of any of the lenses. They're like a 'Spectacles Through the Ages' display in a second-rate museum. Because he couldn't tell you when his last eye test was, the consensus was that it was a fairly safe bet that none of them were giving him 20 20 vision.

I first clocked that his glasses probably weren't right when he came to my house and seemed to struggle with his vision. My husband and I were sitting in the garden reading the papers when dad appeared at the side gate, as he often did, on his way to the pub.

"Only me!" he announced proudly. Sorting a chair in the garden for him, we chatted amiably for a while.

Picking up a newspaper he moved it nearer and further from his face as though trying to focus in.

"Dad, do you think you need to have your eyes tested?" I asked.

He looked at me as though I was daft, shook his head and replied, "No!"

"I think maybe you do" I replied. "I can take you. It's no problem."

I nipped off up to the house to fetch him a beer and on my return discovered he'd taken off the offending glasses.

Handing him his drink I asked, "Where are your glasses, dad?"

He looked at me defiantly as if to say, "what glasses?"

I began to laugh, "Dad, just because you've taken them off, it doesn't mean I have forgotten that you wear them. You can put them back on now."

Like a child who has been chastised, he fetched his glasses out of the pocket he had hidden them in and plonked them sulkily back on his nose.

Placing his drink on the table, he wrinkled his nose as if trying to remember something. His face jolted with a spark of recognition, and he announced proudly, "I was in the Working Men's Club until 4 o'clock this morning!"

Laughing, my husband replied, "Did you have a lock in George?"

To which dad retorted, "No, they didn't lock me in – I wanted to stay!"

About an hour later after he'd enjoyed a beer in the sunshine, he made moves to be on his way, and ambled off to have a pint in town.

An appointment at an optician in town was made, and I duly picked him up and took him on the day. Well, I say that I picked him up and took him, like you can just 'pick him up and take him'. What really happened was this:

I called down a couple of days before and marked the appointment on the calendar – he has a big desk calendar which sits next to the big clock calendar, and he crosses off each day. It's the only way he can remember what day he's on.

Next step was to ring him the night before.

"Dad, I'm picking you up tomorrow to take you to have your eyes tested".

He struggles getting his words out, so I give him a couple of moments. Dad replies, "Why's that then?"

"Because everyone has to have their eyes tested, to make sure they have the right glasses" I continued, "I'll pick you up at 1 o'clock, so don't go out, and wait in for me.

"Alright" he says, before hanging up.

The next morning, I sent a Whatsapp message to the carers who pop in on him each morning. Well, that's each *weekday* morning, as he'd taken to wandering off for a walk at the weekend, and they could never get in. They spent more time on his doorstep and messaging us on the group, than actually being able to get inside to do their job, so we cancelled them.

Me: Please can you ask dad not to go out, and be ready to leave the house at 1 o'clock when I'll pick him up for his eye test

At 12:45 I ring his house number. He picks up, and his voice sounds wheedley, "hello?".

My first thought is relief as he's actually at home and we don't have to now play the increasingly more frequent 'Hunt the dad' game.

"Hi dad, it's Lynnette – are you alright?"

"Yes" … he seems puzzled why I ask.

I continue, "I'm leaving my house now, to pick you up at 1 o'clock. Can you get your shoes on, and get ready to come with me?"

"Where are we going?"

My inner demon pipes up, "It's like blooming Groundhog Day!"

Silencing her, I try not to let the frustration I'm feeling creep into my voice, and carry on cheerfully, "For an eye test dad – remember I told you? It's on the calendar".

I hear shuffling, and I know that he's having a look at said calendar.

"Oh," he replies, then "Why's that then?"

"Because everyone has to have one, to make sure they have the right glasses, and that they work properly. I'll be down in a minute to fetch you".

By the time I've driven the short ride across town to dad's house, I'm mentally steeling myself for the fun packed afternoon ahead of me. It's not dad's fault, but everything takes much longer and there are literally hours of my life that I am never going to see again. When he answers the door, I'm relieved to see that he's got his shoes on and is ready to go.

"Have you got everything you need?" I ask. "Wallet? Keys?"

He pats down his pockets, looking pleased with himself when he pulls out his wallet at the first pocket guess.

Replacing it back, he gives it another pat to reassure himself that it's still there.

"Keys?" I continue.

Reaching into his trouser pocket, he's even more pleased to locate his keys, and by now is grinning like a kid who's found a great big bag of sweets that he'd forgotten all about.

"Brilliant", I say. "Let's get going then, shall we?"

We lock up the house and shuffle up the drive to the car.

Opening the passenger door, he slowly gets in, and I feed him the seatbelt over his shoulder. This, I've found saves valuable minutes, as I then don't have to remind him to buckle up while he faffs around trying to plug the seatbelt in. By the time I've got in the driver's seat, he's all safely in the car, and off we go.

Dad sometimes gets frustrated that his day-to-day conversations are getting more difficult, as he can't seem to find the words. Sometimes he'll tail off mid flow, and if you give him a moment, he'll sometimes get back on track, but very often the thread has gone off into the ether. Whilst he sometimes can't find any words, he CAN still read. If we're waiting in the Drs, he'll read all the posters and notices, if we are driving in the car, he'll read all the road signs. Out. Loud. All. Of. The. Time.

The optician's appointment involves reading letters of reducing sizes, projected on the wall. As soon as the first set of letters flashed up, his eyes widened with a jolt of recognition, and it was as though someone had plugged him in. He turned his head to the letters and rather excitedly rceled them off, "A Z R K".

Next set of letters, he gets a tad louder "H G D A".

By the time the third set flashes up, he's having a grand old time! He's found something he's good at, after all these times where he's hunted around in his head for the words, here they are. Right here, on the wall! Right in front of his very eyes! Excited now, he's out to impress the optician. His confidence grows, as he shows her once and for all that he is *brilliant* at this game.

He starts singing the letters, like the old 'ABC' song "P W S J"!

The rest of the appointment carried on with the letters flashing up and dad belting them out with gusto – he was having the afternoon of his life! This was the best trip out ever! When the test was all over, we discovered that, surprise surprise, he did indeed need new glasses, and we were shown to the counter to order them.

The next challenge was picking the frames; I swear the ones he had were from the 1970s (or maybe Noah had been a previous owner?), and probably could fetch a few bob on the antique market.

We decide to go for bifocals, as he already wears this sort and is used to them. And opted for a similar size frame as he already wears, as they will be kind of familiar and might stand a fighting chance of not ending up in the bin, with dad thinking they didn't belong to him. Picking a modern frame for the prescription, the optician asks him to try them on for size. Clutching his 70's horn rims in his sweaty palms, he pops the frames on.

Peering out from behind them he squinted, "These are no good", he says. "Can't see bugger all out of them!"

Smiling to myself, I countered, "These are just the frames, dad. They put your new lenses in them and then you have brand new glasses."

Defiantly putting his old glasses back on, he continues:

"I've got glasses. I can see". "Look – I can see through the top, and" To the amusement of the sales assistant, he flings his head back dramatically, and squints through the bottom lens, "I can see through the bottom. I don't need new glasses".

Realising that there's no point in arguing, and that he will have forgotten the conversation a few minutes after anyway, I reply, "OK dad, pop your glasses back on, we'll go home now."

When the new glasses arrive, I'll take them down and he'll hopefully have a 'blind man can see' miracle moment, and I can secretly squirrel his antique collection out of the house. Although that might have to be done in stages, so he doesn't spend the next few weeks driving himself mad looking for them.

Making our way back towards the car, I noticed that his hair could do with a trim. Dad's Army background means that his hair is always neat and tidy, and he prides himself on being smart – he always wears a shirt and tie, and I don't think ever in his life has he ever owned a pair of jeans.

"Shall we get you a quick haircut while we're in town?" I ask.

His disappointed expression tells me that he thinks I think he looks scruffy, and he touches his silver hair. "Do I need one?" he asks.

"Only at the back, I gently say, "and then only a little trim".

He looks reassured by this, and we amble slowly to the nearest Barber's.

It's a sit and wait your turn place, and big leather couch dominates the front window, with a wooden chair beside. There's one man ahead of us in the queue. As I sloshed down into the couch, I gestured to dad to take the chair. It was obvious to me that if he got ensconced into this couch, there was no way he was getting out unassisted. He picks up a newspaper and has a flick through. There was a time where he'd practically read the print off a newspaper, but nowadays he just seems to flick through the headlines and look at the pictures. It's blatantly obvious that he hasn't a clue what the stories are about, he's just going through the motions of reading the paper.

Carefully folding and placing the paper back on the table, he takes in his surroundings. It's a big, modern barber shop with bright lights and big shiny mirrors. Six chairs with customers line the outside walls: three each side. Spotting the man nearest to us having a super short buzz cut all over, dad homed in on him and stared intently. A worried expression passes through his face, and I know exactly what he's thinking.

"You don't have to have that haircut, dad. His is only that short because that's what he wants". I continue, "You can just have a trim like you normally do."

Shaking his head, he replied, "no".

"What do you mean, no?" I countered.

Dad quickly gets up out of the chair, and heads for the door.

I take that as a sure sign that he doesn't want a haircut after all. By this time, there's no point in arguing, and as I roll my eyes to the man ahead of us in the queue, as we've just wasted 20 minutes in there, we leave.

Driving back towards dad's house, he points directly at a barber shop on the right.

"That's where I go!" he says, excitedly. "There!"

By now, there's no turning back, so I resignedly park the car, and we enter the shop. This particular barber has been in business since anyone can remember, and it's like stepping back in time. With just two seats in front of the large mirror, the plugs for the trimmers hang from the ceiling and the tiles on the walls are circa 1950. For the two chairs, patched together with black duct tape, there is only one barber. My heart sinks slightly when I clock there are three more before us in the queue – there was no chance this is going to be a quick in and out job. The barber gives dad a cheery welcome and we sit down and wait our turn.

Dad sits contentedly beside me, drinking in the surroundings and I could feel him visibly relax. He used to come here as a young man and I can see that this is all familiar, and he feels safe here. I try to shut my inner demon off, who was screaming, "For GOD'S SAKE! It's been three hours since we left his house. THREE HOURS! When did an eye appointment take THREE WHOLE HOURS? Time we will never get back!".

Sensible me reasoned that there were worse ways to spend an afternoon and after all, we're kind of stuck here now so we had to make the most of it. The barber was full of banter and a bit of a crowd pleaser; the jokes were flying around the place thick and fast. When it was dad's turn, Chris the barber called over, "You're next, George me old son". Dad made his way slowly to the chair and got cloaked up.

"Still playing the trumpet?", to which Chris held an imaginary trumpet and waggled his fingers as though playing it. Dad smiles, and nods.

"You'll have to bring it up and play us a tune", he continues, with another trumpet playing impression. "I will!" says dad, proudly.

Chris the barber then conducts a one-sided conversation, and I noticed that the only answers dad had to provide were yes or no, or at worse a nod or shake of the head would suffice. Realising that Chris knew dad from old and was well aware that he wasn't completely the man he used to be, I silently thanked him for preserving dad's dignity and pride, and making his hair cut an enjoyable experience.

Whipping off the cloak and brushing the stray hairs off dad's neck, he announced "That'll be £5.50, young man!" At this point dad seemed to go into autopilot. His hand went straight to his pocket and located his wallet first time. He whipped it out, took out a ten-pound note, paid up and put the change back.

Looking in the mirror approvingly, he puffed up his chest and walked over to where I was still sitting.

"That's better" he said, with a smile.

*I Dad as a child*

A few days later, nipping in to check on dad, I noticed he was poring through his latest bank statement, and had his debit card out on the side table.

Seeing him looking through his statement reminded me of a time when I was a really small child.

*"Where are you going dad?"*

*"I'm going to work".*

*"But why do you have to go to work? Stay here and play with me".*

*Dad replied, "I can't stay at home, I have to go to work".*

*"Why…" I wheedled… "Why do you have to go to work?"*

*"To get pennies" was his reply.*

*At this point, life to me made perfect sense, and I really couldn't believe my dad could be so silly!*

*"You don't need to go to work to get pennies… just go to the bank like you always do!"*

Going back to the bank statement of present day, I took a covert glance over it to make sure it all looked in order, as it's always a worry that he'll get taken in by someone, or someone will ask him for money. He's forever losing his wallet and its contents, so we need to be extra vigilant.

"You need to help me", he says.

"What with?"

"Buy a car". To this, my inner demon shouted, "Over my dead body!", but sensible me replied calmly, "You can't have a car dad, you're not allowed".

His body visibly stiffened, his eyes hardened, and a determined look crossed his face. "Who said?", he challenged. He reached for his driving licence, turned it over, and jabbed his finger at the little pictures of vehicles on the back. "This says…I can." He added, insolently.

Officially, his driving licence hasn't been taken away, but after he crashed his car in a ditch thinking that he could drive home from Scotland in a blizzard, then had a minor crash with another car shortly after that, we'd taken the family decision to preserve his life (and that of others) and remove his car. At the time we told him that my sister's son needed to borrow it as his own car was broken and he needed to get to work. Thinking he was helping his Grandson out, dad handed over the keys willingly and we stored the car on my sister's drive while working out what to actually do with it. A few months later after a meal out for dad's birthday, we all ended up heading back to my sister's house to continue the party there. On arrival dad spotted the car and a spark of recognition flashed in his eyes. Pursing his lips, he approached the car, circling around it curiously.

Pointing at the offending vehicle, he said, "Mine!". As a family huddled together on the drive, we all collectively had a sharp intake of breath, not knowing quite what to do until my nephew saved the day.

"Yes Grandad, it looks like your old car doesn't it! I got one just like yours!"

Dad mulled this over and nodded. We all slowly exhaled and looked guiltily at one another.

Back to dad wanting a new car, I told him yet another white lie.

"The Doctor said you can't have another car. Because you sometimes can't remember things, he was worried you would get lost." Watching cautiously as he digested this information, I was relieved when he didn't come back with a counter argument.

At this point I noticed his wallet was on the side with all the cards taken out. I had a quick look inside – it was empty. Slightly alarming, as only a few days earlier, he'd had some £10 and £20 notes in there, and he hadn't been anywhere to spend any money.

"Where's your money, dad?", to which he pulled a face and shrugged.

Inner demon piped up, "Brilliant! Now let's play 'hunt the house out' to see what he's done with it. Marvellous!"

Sensible me said, "Remember when you lost your wallet before, and we found it in your pant drawer? I'll pop upstairs and see if I can find it."

Upstairs, I started the systematic search, as lost items are seldom found in the same place twice. In the back bedroom there's a wardrobe with all dad's military clothes, his mess kit, his greens and his best coats. Going through all the pockets, I felt an unfamiliar lump in his overcoat. Pulling it out revealed his burgundy para beret, last seen at the previous Remembrance Parade.

By this point, dad had made his way upstairs and was standing at the doorway. Happily, I waved the beret at him.

"Remember when we went to the parade?"

Dad cocked his head to one side, scrunched his nose in thought and slowly nodded.

I continued slowly to allow him time to locate the memory. "And we went to the pub after …and you thought someone had stolen your beret?"

I could see this was slowly coming back to him. He nodded.

"Well, look at this! You'd put it in your pocket of all places!"

Handing the beret to him, his face broke out into a wide smile. Turning to the mirror, he smoothed down his hair, positioned the beret on his head and stood to attention.

Leaving him to admire his reflection, I continued the search.

A quick root round the front bedroom located a zip up bag inside a cupboard, and inside were his bank books and the missing money. Relieved, I called out,

"Found it dad, panic over," I trilled. "It was in this bag – look - you'd put it in a safe place with your other bank bits". I continued, "Panic over!"

At this, I zipped up the bag and returned it to where I'd found it.

Joining me in the front bedroom, dad said, "They come up here and move things!"

"Who?

"The people". I thought for a while and then I realised what he was trying to tell me.

We'd arranged for a company of carers to call in on dad each day to keep an eye on him and tidy round.

"Ahh the carer people? They don't come up here to move things, they're changing your bed and stuff".

He's adamant by now, "No, they come and move things. AND they go and have a shit in the toilet!"

"They don't do that dad; they're cleaning your bathroom and taking your washing down" Inner demon is currently clutching her sides with laughter.

He was determined now, and continued, "No, you listen! They come and have a shit in my toilet!"

At this, my inner demon pipes up, "Pretty sure they don't! I can't think of anything worse!" She then does a weird fake gagging noise, before helplessly dissolving into peals of laughter, dispersed with snorting, "shit…. In the toilet!"

Knowing there is no sense at all in continuing the discussion, as it's the absolute truth in dad's mind, sensible me looks at him and says, "They honestly go in there to clean round, but I'll ask them not to use the toilet."

He seems pacified by that.

After a long career in the Army, dad's always been an active man. He walks everywhere and used to take great pride in telling you exactly how many minutes it took him to walk to the pub (exactly seven if you were wondering).

He even signed up to a half marathon to 'give him something to work for' in his 40s. Nowadays his knees are playing up a bit, and he's just not as fast as he used to be, which he finds frustrating.

He's taken to a daily walk around the park next to his road, "to keep things moving". One day I'd walked down to see him, so accompanied him on his walk as it was on my way home.

The park looked beautiful for the time of year, with all the plants bursting into life from their winter slumber. The sun was shining, and the setting was perfect.

Dad ambled slowly along the bottom path, as was his daily route, turning left by the pitch and putt, then left again. Noticing he was struggling a touch, up a slight incline, I offered my hand to support him. He waved it away, gesturing that he could manage just fine, thank you. I asked him if his knees were painful, and he nodded with a look of annoyance.

He turned off the path into the bandstand area of the park and plonked himself down on the bench. Patting the space next to him for me, I joined him. "I sit here", he said.

We sat together in contented silence, looking down towards the bandstand, with only the sounds of the birds singing and the leaves rustling in the trees keeping us company. I got the impression this was his daily routine, and part of his day that he really loved. He looked peaceful, soaking up the sights and sounds.

"It's beautiful" I replied.

We sat there for a good while, enjoying the peace and quiet, needing no words or conversation.

When it was time for me to return to work, I checked he had his key and would be safe to get home and hugged him goodbye.

On returning home I called his doctor to make an appointment for them to look at his knees, just to see if anything underlying was wrong with them.

A couple of days later, I picked him up and took him to the surgery. Sitting in the waiting room, dad's reading all the posters around the place. It's his way of compensating for the frustrating silences when he tries to have a conversation, proving to himself that the words are still in there. Somewhere.  In due course, we're called through.

The doctor asked what the problem seemed to be, and I explained that his knees seemed stiff and a bit swollen. I added that he's had cellulitis in the past and a knee drain after a fall, so this visit was just a precaution that nothing had returned. She asked dad to pop his trousers off and jump on to the bench.

At this point I hoped fervently that he had clean pants, or indeed, any pants on at all.

Laying back on the bench, the doctor begins her examination.

"When I press here, do you feel pain?"

"No"

She continues, "Here? Here? Here?" Each time, the answer was no from dad.

Inner demon rolled her eyes and said "He could hardly move the other day, and said his knees were painful. Brilliant – now we look like a pair of timewasters bleeding the NHS's already strapped resources".

Oh, but dad wasn't finished there… oh no, indeed. Of course there was more!

The doctor asked if he could bend his legs, and dad was up for the challenge. Almost as though he was training for his next half marathon, those legs came up one by one, bending almost to his chest. Dad's looking mightily pleased with himself. "Look!" his eyes said, "Look at how far I can get my knees to bend!"

Inner demon snorted, "Flipping 'eck! He's like Grandpa Joe from Willy Wonka! Lay in bed for 20 years then jumped around like a teenager when the golden ticket showed up!".

The doctor laughed and asked him to put his trousers back on and turned to me.

I knew before the words even came out what was coming next.

"There's nothing wrong with your dad's knees, they are just getting old". She continued, "I'll give him some ibuprofen gel that he can rub in, and just get some ibuprofen tablets from the chemist too. That should sort the stiffness and swelling.

Now this is easier said than done. Gel is fine. Tablets not so much. If he has tablets in the cupboard, who's to say he won't take too many, or forget that he's had any, or when? Not take any at all? Eat them all in one go? The possibilities arc endless!

We know this from bitter experience.

Dad only takes two tablets a day, which we are eternally grateful that it's not a bigger number. One for memory (obviously not working) and one for a past prostate problem. Two tablets taken both together, first thing in the morning is almost manageable; God knows what he'd be like if he had to take any more, or ones at different times of the day. In a word, we'd be stuffed.

He used to keep the two boxes in the pantry, and diligently take one pill out of each, every morning. Visiting one day, I had a quick look in the pantry to see if he needed a repeat order. Not a tablet in sight.

"Where are your pills, dad?"

His reply was a blank expression that I've come to call his 'Buggered if I know' face. It's the one that's trying to process firstly 'what tablets' and secondly a slight roll of his eyes and a purse of his lips. After a thorough search of the kitchen the pill boxes were finally found and were completely empty. Another hunt around the kitchen revealed a matchbox on the shelf containing all his pills plus a couple of leftover antibiotic tablets from his knee drain.

Ahhh that makes perfect sense, dad… not!

"Dad, why have you put all the pills in here?". He looked genuinely confused as to why on earth would he have done such a thing.

I continued, "Now we don't know what tablets you have, and what you haven't".

He peered into the matchbox and looked at me. Tapping the side of his head, he said, "It's this!", continuing with "It's going like my dad's!"

Looking back Grandad must have had Alzheimer's too. I'm not sure if it was a clear diagnosis, but there were definite similarities.

Because we now had absolutely no way of knowing if and when he'd taken his tablets, it was time to make some changes. We arranged for his pills to be delivered direct from the pharmacy, instead of dad having to collect them. This meant that they were already sorted into dosset pouches that he just had to pierce each day. This seemed like a perfect solution, until…

Message from the carers: "It's Tuesday, and George looks like he's taken his tablets up to Saturday". This could well be the case, or because the tablets are delivered monthly, he might not have had any since last Saturday…nobody will ever know. It's a mystery that will never be solved.

We then arranged for them to be delivered weekly instead of monthly. This way, if he does happen to get out of synch, it's only for a couple of days, and it's impossible for him to take a whole month's worth by mistake.

I realised little by little we are having to make more and more adjustments to accommodate his illness.

2 Playing his trumpet

Because dad's started losing his keys (along with many other items including wallets, money and his memory), I arranged for someone from the Assisted Technology team to come out for a visit. There are many things available to help people. On a previous visit, they had provided him with a big dementia-friendly clock and calendar, and an ingenious clock that reminded him (in my voice) to take his tablets at 10am each morning. I think the talking clock may have confused him though, as it went missing one day, never to return: probably in landfill somewhere yakking away to itself every morning.

The door knocked and a friendly-looking lady stood on the drive. I ushered her inside.

Noting that dad was looking her up and down warily as she was an unfamiliar face, I reassured him that it was safe to allow her into the house. Entering the lounge, we all took a seat. After the pleasantries and introductions, she began to speak:

"So, George, I'm here to see if I can give you some goodies that will make things easier for you".

At this, he seemed to visibly relax. I'm pretty sure that the words 'give' and 'goodies' had landed well. Despite not being short of money, getting him to part with any is a challenge in itself. Because I take his shopping down to him and fill up the fridge, I'm convinced he thinks I'm an ace daughter who pays for everything.

*Spoiler alert, not true. I transfer the money back from his account straight afterwards. I used to take him shopping but it always turned out to be an all-day event. He'd be counting the slices in the loaves of bread to make sure he got the one with the most in. I'd put things in the trolley to turn around and find he'd put them back. By me doing his shopping saves literally hours of time and has the added bonus that I could put him some goodies and treats in there without him questioning the price of them or putting them back on the shelf.

Taking a seat in the lounge, Buonita introduced herself, and asked first if he manages to use the phone. The 'buggered if I know' face says, 'what phone?'. I interject and explain that he does have numbers stored in his phone, but he struggles with pressing QuickDial then the number. By the time he's figured which buttons to press, the line times out.

With this information, she whips out a new phone with big buttons, which will be ideal for him. "George," she says "this phone will help you with that. We can store your numbers in there and you only need to press one button to make a call.

"And" she continued, "If someone is calling you, their button will flash so you'll know who it is."

The phone looks absolutely what he needs, and she proceeds to write down the six numbers he might want to ring the most. With Buonita busy programming the phone up and making labels for the six big buttons on the front, I feel like we're making progress.

With all the labels in place, Buonita continued, "Where's your dad's phone socket?".

I gestured to the sockets under the front window.

"And where's the nearest plug socket to that?"

A quick scan around the room revealed the nearest socket wasn't near at all – it was on the other side of the room.

"Hmmm" Buonita mused. "The phone needs a power socket near to the phone socket".

I knew there'd be a snag in the master plan. Why on earth I thought it would be a simple operation, I do not know.

"Not to worry" she trills. "We can have a practice for now, but the phone lead will have to be extended. We can't have the wires trailing all over the place. We don't want you to trip over them, do we George?" she said, patting his arm.

Buonita then proceeds to explain how the phone works.

"All you have to do now is pick up the receiver and press the name of the person you want to call". She continued, "So George, let's have a practice" Buonita says. "Let's try to ring Lynnette".

Momentarily a confused expression passes over his face. He looks at me, "That's you?"

"Yes" I reply and nodded quickly.

"OK then George... pick up the phone".

Slowly he picks up the handset. "Now press 'Lynnette'. Slowly, his finger hovers over my button, then he jabs it. In a few moments, my phone begins to ring. Waving my phone happily at dad and pointing to the screen to show him my phone told me it was him ringing, I press 'Answer'.

"Hello!" I said into the receiver. Momentarily he looks confused as I am both here in the room and in his phone, I continued. "It's me dad. That's my number. If you need to talk to me just press that button and my little phone will ring." I concluded, "That's good, isn't it?"

Dad looks pleased with himself.

This new technology might take a bit of practice, but I really do think he'll get the hang of it.

For the moment though, until we can extend the phone cord and make the wires safe, back in its box it went.

Buonita continues with her bag of goodies. "How are you with finding keys?"

Inner demon snorts "Crap!". I answer "Not so good – he loses them quite a bit, or forgets which pocket they are in.

"Then I have just the thing for you!" She whips out a box. Inside were four coloured key ring fobs labelled A to D and a remote control.

"We can put these onto your keys, and if you lose them, we can press the remote control, and your keys will whistle". She explained.

A remote control that can be aligned to fobs on keys. Perfect!

"Where are your house keys, George?"

He stands up and starts to pat down his pockets one by one. He takes out his wallet and opens it slowly, revealing loose change within, but no keys.

Inner demon has her head in her hands, "I don't believe it! I sincerely do not believe this is happening."

The next half an hour is spent searching coat pockets, trouser pockets, random wallets and drawers to locate the missing keys. He should have two sets. Eventually, one set is found in the tub of random keys in the kitchen... why didn't we look there first? Buonita pops the red Fob A on the keys and synchs it to the remote.

"Let's have a little practice, George," she said. "If you lose your keys now, we can just press this red button, and it will find them for you." She duly pressed the red button on the remote control, and as if by magic, the keys in dad's hand began to vibrate and whistle. Dad looked at them in surprise and smiled.

We do the same with the garage key and she then instructed me to put the remote somewhere dad wouldn't think of looking. The device is useless without the remote, and if he found it, it's highly likely he'd either forget what it was for, take it to pieces, hide it or it would go the same way as that talking clock.

Two hours after Buonita had arrived for her one-hour appointment, she bade us goodbye and went off to her next call.

I'm sure she's well used to this kind of thing, but I really do hope Buonita doesn't think we are a family of complete idiots.

The next day I arrived at dad's in plenty of time to pick him up for the Veteran's coffee morning. This is a monthly event that he really enjoys. Organised by our local council and an organisation called Joining Forces, it's a great place that welcomes any ex-service people and their families to meet up for a natter. Added to that they have useful resources and advice for older people; it was there we found out about Attendance Allowance, a benefit you can claim towards carer's fees, which we'd never heard of previously.

I officially volunteer at the Veteran's coffee morning that's held in a hall in the town centre. Working for the NHS, permission can be granted if your cause aligns with NHS Values. The coffee mornings are a great place for older people to meet and chat, so it didn't take much convincing on the grounds of combating loneliness and improving the lives of older people. My volunteer work there serves two purposes. One, it's a great initiative and the veterans are a lovely bunch of people; two, it allows me to keep an eye on dad to make sure he's safe and doesn't wander off and make a break for the pub.

Arriving nice and early and armed with a hammer and cable tacks, I planned to make the phone wire safe while dad got ready for the coffee morning, factoring a little extra time in for the inevitable last-minute faffing around routine.

Knocking on the door, there was no answer. Noticing the curtain upstairs twitch I was relieved that 1) he was up and 2) he'd seen me. Giving him a couple of minutes to make his way down the stairs, I saw his shape approach the inner front door. Then I saw it leave again. With a sinking feeling I guessed that he'd lost his keys and was now shuffling around the house to try to find them. The key finder was useless at this point as he didn't know where the remote was, and I couldn't get in to activate it. After what seemed like an age, he reappeared and unlocked the door. Hooray! He opened the door and let me in.

"It's Veteran's coffee morning today, Dad. Why don't you get your shoes on, and then we can go?" He headed off back upstairs, and I busied myself with hooking the phone line over the doorframe and tacking it round. Plugging it in, it surged into life and all the little lights came on the display. Pleased with myself at getting the phone working, I realised he was still upstairs. Probably finding a tie, I thought. Using this time, I quickly made him a plate of sandwiches, pork pie and cake, and put it in the fridge for him to eat later for his tea.

Going back into the hallway, there was still no sign of him.

"Dad!" I called "Where are you? Are you OK"?

A barely audible "Yes" floated down the stairs. Looking at my watch I realised we would soon need to get a wriggle on, as time was ticking by. Mounting the stairs, I found him in the back room with two outfits laid out on the bed. One was his Army Greens and the other was his full Mess Kit, and he gently touched them each in turn, as though deciding which to wear.

Both were way over dressed for a coffee morning, so I softly said "You don't need those dad, it's not a parade or anything" I went into his room and found his Para Beret and his Airborne tie and took them back to him.

"These will do just perfectly, Dad. Let me put your uniforms away."

Seeing his Mess Kit laying on the bed took me back to a time where he wasn't this man who stood before me. Who wasn't this confused person, who frustrated everyone – but mostly himself – with his lack of memory and ability to lose objects on a daily basis.

*"Are you lonesome tonight, do you miss me tonight, are you sorry we drifted apart". The song boomed out of the bathroom where dad was shaving. He continued singing "Does your memory stray, to that bright summer's day, when you kissed me and called me sweetheart".*

*Dad was always clean-shaven, well apart from that time when he grew that god-awful moustache in the early 80s – which thankfully had a short life.*

*Ablutions over, he'd then put on his full Mess Kit; red jacket, dark trousers with a red stripe down the side. He used to love the Mess dos. He'd proudly enter the lounge in full attire, then the little suit brusher would appear. A fuzzy little gadget that brushed the fluff off your clothes. Us kids weren't allowed within spitting distance of the fuzzy brush. It worked perfectly if you brushed in the right direction, but if you got it slightly in the wrong direction it dumped all the fluff back onto the clothes. Something we didn't want to be part of just before his big night out. The mess dos were the height of the social calendar; Mam and dad dressed up in their finest clothes, and from the level of singing and giggling we heard on their return, we gathered they were a great night out.*

*My mam would sew her own ballgowns for the Mess do, always with a matching zip up clutch bag to carry her cigarettes and lipstick.*

*My step mum after would pride herself in finding flamboyant long dresses in the local charity shops. I got the impression early on that it really wasn't good form to turn up in the same dress twice, so both had their own ways of playing along to the etiquette.*

*Dad would puff his chest out, and boom "Come on then, my sweetheart". He'd put a protective arm around his wife's shoulders, and they'd leave for the party.*

*In the early days, this left my brother and I free to watch old horror films, hiding under his stripy dressing gown, and in later year I would be trusted to babysit my younger brother and sister. Well, when I say 'babysit' I actually mean 'pack them off to bed early so I could watch Dynasty in peace'.*

Yes, that man with his booming voice and love of a great party was a world apart from the one who stood before me.

"Come on then dad, let's be having you" I said.

Reaching the front door, I asked if he had his keys to lock up. He pulled out a little zip up wallet, opened it up and I spotted there were now two sets of keys in there. The missing ones from yesterday had turned up. He then patted his other pocket and almost seemed surprised that his wallet was in there. Locking up, we left his house and headed off to the coffee morning.

Arriving at the hall, I settled dad down at a table, then began my stint making sure everyone had a drink and chatting to them. Each time I got to dad's table, he told them proudly, "She's mine, she is – she's my daughter". By the end of the morning, I'm pretty sure that nobody on that table or indeed in the room was in any doubt who I was or whom I belonged to!

After the coffee morning, I took dad home. Once we were safely in, I put the other key finder fob on the miraculously re-appeared keys and synched the remote from its hiding place under the stairs. I then warmed him a hot meal for his lunch and laid it out on his table.

Feeling accomplished that the phone worked, we'd had a trip out, his lunch and tea were sorted, and we'd be able to find his keys if needed, I told him I had to go, and that he needed to lock up after me then go and eat his lunch. On the doorstep, he starts,

"Now then. How do I get…" he tails off, searching his mind for the right word… "MONEY".

Inner demon's and my heart sank together. No, this can't be right. What NOW?

"Dad," I reminded him. Your wallet was in that pocket. You showed me this morning. I pointed to said pocket.

He patted his pocket, pulled out his wallet, opened it up and to my dismay it was empty.

Puzzled, I said, "You had money in there the other day. Where is it?"

Shaking his head, he looked imploringly with an expression that simply said, "I have no idea".

I whizzed upstairs to have a quick look in the usual places, and the random assortment of wallets were still in random places, but none of them contained the bank notes I'd seen a few days back.

Returning downstairs, I said "Don't worry dad. You eat your lunch and I'll fetch you some money and bring it back". He looked relieved at this idea. It's not that he goes anywhere really to need any money, more that he's always had some in his wallet and feels a bit lost if there's none there. Like he's got nothing to spend it on, but if he DID want to, he likes to feel that he can.

Returning a while later with the replacement money for his wallet, I handed him £30 in fivers, thinking that if the other money turned up (which it definitely will at some point), we'd know which money was which.

Carefully putting the money in his wallet, he returned the wallet to his trouser pocket and patted it gently, reassuring himself it was safe.

Chapter 6

On the subject of money I was reminded of a family holiday in Cornwall when we were children.

*For many years, we had our family holidays at the Lizard in Cornwall. Each year, dad would pack up the roof rack, then put the back car seats down. A makeshift bed would be made, and myself and my younger sister and brother would settle off to sleep. Dad always drove through the night, and we'd set off around 9 in the evening. Like magic, when we woke up, we were on holiday!*

*The holiday chalet consisted of just three rooms. A back bedroom for mum, dad and our baby brother, a middle kitchen diner and a front living room with a sofa bed where my sister and I slept. There was no bathroom, so it was strip washes in the kitchen, and the toilet was outside. Having no television meant the only evening entertainment was scrutinising a picture in the lounge of the Cornish coastline and trying to make as many animals as possible out of the shapes of the rocks. The lawnmower was in the shape of a horse called Little Boy (who was far from little!) who used to roam loose in the garden to eat the grass.*

*Each morning, dad would boom, "Where to, today?"*

*My sister and I would glance at each other, and we knew what we both were thinking, "Let it be Flambards, let it be Flambards!" another glance out of the window would confirm to us that it definitely would NOT be Flambards! Flambards was a small theme park a few miles up the road, and we only ever went there if it happened to rain.*

*With Flambards out of the question, Dad would go out into the garden to study the cloud situation. With the Lizard being the most southerly point in Britain, he had a theory that the area had its very own microclimate, and he had a very scientific method for forecasting the weather (not!). This involved him facing towards what would be the Lizard Point, then studying the sky to see where the clouds were. Glancing again at each other, my sister and I prayed silently, "Kynance". Kynance was a beach to the west of the point, reached by a beautiful clifftop walk; us all walking and our little brother in a carrier on dad's back; and a stunning stone path descent to the beach. When the tide was out, there were brilliant waves to play in, rock pools to explore and fine sand to run about on. Whichever cliff top walk we ended up on, it was a standing joke that at some point dad would whip out his imaginary telescope, point it out to sea and proclaim, "I see no ships, only hardships".*

*In the other direction was Cadgewith, which is a beautiful fishing village full of thatched cottages. But the beach was shingly and, in our minds, boring. Added to that, it was FLIPPING MILES to walk to.*

*Dad looked undecided on the cloud situation that particular day.*

*"Right then!" He announced. "I think we'll go in the car to St Ives."*

*My sister and I looked at each other in disbelief. We could hardly contain our excitement. We were going in the car! To a proper seaside resort – with shops, and everything!*

*Once there, I was keen to escape the family.*

*"Dad, can I go and have a look round the shops?"*

*My little sister, five years my junior piped up "can I come too?".*

*I was at the age where I was just coming into my teen years, and definitely didn't want HER trailing around with me. I was hip, I was cool in my button-down skirt and new T shirt – and she would most definitely destroy the image I had in my mind of me swanning around the seaside shops, being a grown up.*

*"Yes, you can go with her" was the reply. I pulled a face, but the deal was done. I was stuck with her for the afternoon.*

*"I'll give you some spending money". Now this undeniably softened the blow. A bit of spendies took the sting off having my little sister trailing round with me for the afternoon a little. Dad whipped a pound note out of his wallet, carefully ripped it in half and handed one half to each of us. Looking pleased with himself, he announced,*

*"Now you can spend it when you've decided what you really want, and not on the first thing you see". Looking pleased at his own ingenuity he continued, "AND you won't lose each other!"*

A couple of days after the Veteran's Coffee Morning, I popped in on dad to drop his shopping off.

It was a glorious day, the sun was beating down, and life was good. To top off the good mood feeling, dad answered the door – which he'd remembered to lock – on the first rat-a-tat-tat on the door. With a spring in my step, I entered his kitchen, unpacked all the shopping and felt a teeny bit smug to note that the fridge was all full again, and he had supplies for the week ahead.

"How are you dad?" I asked.

"Alright" was the response.

"Been anywhere?" He pulled a face, and said "no, not really". I followed him into the lounge and as we entered the hot air in there practically took the skin off my face. Inner demon proclaimed, "Christ on a bike, it's like a sauna in here!"

Looking at his mock electric log burner, I noticed that the flickering firelight was on, and the fan heaters were blasting away. In addition, he'd plugged in another small fan heater next to his chair, and that was merrily blasting away too.

Refusing to spend any money on installing central heating, he had an assortment of fan heaters and electric oil heaters that he wheeled out and used as and when he saw fit.

"Why have you got all the heaters on?" I asked.

"Yes, when it's flipping boiling out there!" chimed inner demon.

Switching off the heaters, I noticed that the big button phone was currently unplugged and lifeless. This was rather worrying, as should he need said phone in any kind of emergency, it wouldn't work.

Inner demon rolled her eyes skywards.

"Why have you unplugged your phone, dad?" I ventured.

The familiar blank expression fleeted across his face as he processed what it was I was asking, then bingo! The moment of clarity. As though it was the most perfectly reasonable answer to the question, and with a look that said, "Is this not obvious?", he answered "To save gas."

"For goodness' sake" snapped inner demon.

"Dad", I reasoned. "The phone won't work if it's not plugged in, and you need it to work in case you have to contact any of us" I continued "And it doesn't use any electricity really".

"Not anywhere as much as having every heater in the house on full whack" added Inner demon.

Plugging the phone in, it sparked back into life.

"There you go," I turned to him. "All working again now!"

"You're a good 'un" he said. I wondered fleetingly how long it might be before he didn't really know WHICH good 'un I was, as he's already started to have to think about my name.

Reminding him to lock the front door behind me, I headed back home, secure in the knowledge that his fridge was full, and the phone was working.

The next day, a message from the carers popped up:

'Front door unlocked, internal door was open, George in conservatory. Phone has been switched off at the wall. Switched it back on again'.

My heart sank. For one, how long had the doors all been open? Just this morning, or all night? Second, why has he unplugged the phone again? He's becoming a danger to himself, and I really don't know what the answer is. It flits through my mind that he won't be able to live alone in the house forever, and a time would come where we would have to make some agonising decisions about where he would live safely in the future. We really have tried to make adjustments, but nothing seems to be quite enough. For a while he had meals on wheels delivered, but as he was never at home to receive the deliveries, these were cancelled, and the daily carers took on the job of heating a microwave meal for him.

At the moment, moving house is completely out of the question, as his old self still steps into his life momentarily. The old self who is stubborn and proud and can absolutely take care of himself. The old self who needs help from nobody. The old self who can think for himself. We don't see the old self very often, or for very long, but he's still there behind dad's confused eyes, and pops out defiantly from time to time.

Maybe we need to put some signs around the place? It's worth a try – ones on the door to remind him to lock them, and ones on the plug near the phone telling him not to unplug it.

*3 Dad and his BSA Gold Flash*

Our youngest brother has a cottage in Scotland and decided to take his children for a holiday there and take dad and Mary along too.

When he told us they were all going away for a week, my first thought was, "He'll love that!"

This was quickly followed by inner demon punching the air. "Yes!" she skipped around. "Yes!... A whole week with NO DAD DRAMAS!"

I must admit, I did resonate with her with this one. One Whole Week. Seven Whole Days. No daily text from the carers telling us that he's unplugged his phone, or left the doors unlocked, or that he's ran out of bread. No quick visits that turn into two-hour events where we're searching his house for the wallet or keys that he's lost. A whole week where we weren't dreading what was going to be in the text we were about to open. One whole week where we could just switch off and relax. Because all said and done, life could be pretty exhausting.

Plus the fact, Dad would have a great time. He'd have a lovely holiday with his wife, son and grandchildren. Everyone was a winner.

*As a small child, I vividly remember family camping holidays. Mam and dad would pile us all in the car and we'd make the journey from Kent up to Yorkshire. I have no idea how they managed to fit four children and all the camping gear into the car, but I'm sure that's another story entirely. Arriving at the camp site, dad would unload the gear and start pitching the tent. My big sister and I would sleep with our parents in the big blue frame tent, and my two elder brothers slept in an old Army bivvy tent next to it. We'd all be given our own airbed to blow up – no pumps back in those days! – and after a somewhat dizzy start, the holiday would begin. With nothing to do but climb down the steep cliff to the beach and climb back up at the end of the day. No club house or holiday park. We'd pick mussels and winkles from the rocks and dad would boil them up on the camping stove for tea. Simple times and happy holidays.*

*In later years when my step mum came along, the family holidays upgraded somewhat, and they bought a caravan. It was probably the smallest caravan in the entire world, but it did the job. Off we went one year down to Devon, Dad, Pat, me and my younger brother and sister. Upon arrival, dad noted the pitch prices and realised that a caravan was the same price with or without an awning, and tents were extra. From this was born a genius plan. He pitched up the old blue tent right next to the caravan, zipped open the porch bit, and flung it over the top of the caravan. Ta da! We now had an awning for the caravan, and dad looked rather pleased with his ingenuity. The holiday went by, with lazy days on the beach, swimming in the sea, and all the usual shenanigans. At the end of the week, the site manager was doing his rounds and collecting the pitch fees, turned to dad and said," One week, one tent, one awning, so that will be X amount".*

*Dad looked at him as though he'd completely lost the plot. He looked pointedly at the shantytown that was our pitch, with the tiny caravan and the tent opening flung across the top of it. He shook his head, and replied, "Tent? There's no tent there – it's clearly an awning."*

*The site manager looked puzzled for a moment, as it clearly wasn't an awning, and was clearly a tent chucked over a caravan. He shook his head, and I think he really hadn't the energy or inclination to argue the toss over a couple of quid – although it was clear that dad was ready and willing for that debate.*

*He crossed something out on the pad, and gave dad a new price for the pitch, and we could tell by the puff of his chest that dad was inwardly congratulating himself on getting away with one.*

*With the site manager out of earshot, dad turned to us beaming from ear to ear and pointed at his head.*

*"Up there for thinking", he said and with a point to his feet and a little jig, "Down there for dancing!"*

*In later years, the holidays upgraded once more with dad and my step mum buying a motor home in the south of France, and later again he and Mary bought various motorhomes and toured all over in them.*

The night before the actual Scotland holiday, my brother phoned dad to say he'd be over in the morning to collect him. As the holiday packing now included three adults, two children, a large dog and two mobility scooters – topped off with an 11-hour drive – my brother had to be super organised. The next morning, he arrived at dad's complete with the car, roof box and trailer. What should have been a half an hour job to load dad's scooter on the trailer and put his case in the car turned into a three-hour marathon. On looking in dad's case, my brother discovered he'd packed a rag tag bundle of dirty clothes. His pyjamas were nowhere to be seen, and quelle surprise, he'd lost his wallet. The wallet situation is veering away from being annoying and is actually getting slightly worrying now. In the past we've found his wallet and money in random places, but now dad sometimes tells us that someone down the road comes into the house. Before, we've told him that it's the carers who come to the house in the morning that come in, but now that we never know if the doors are locked or not, what if someone IS coming into the house?

Dad's also told us that a man down the road says he's going to buy dad's house. In the past we've told him not to be daft… but again, what if there is any truth in it?

Anyway, after a good few hours' delay, eventually they were all on their way, and Scotland-bound. Happily, they arrived late but safe, ready to begin their holiday.

While they were away, my sister and I decided to go into his house and hunt down the missing wallet and money ready for his return. Convinced that people come into the house and move things around, dad's taken to laying out things in his room and putting a towel over the top. First port of call was under all the towels. Nothing there except about five pairs of glasses and an assortment of combs. We then systematically looked in all his drawers. In amongst the piles of junk mail and flyers (which we binned), the first discovery was a collection of bank statements in a wallet, complete with his bank card. In the next drawer down was a plastic box which we opened, and there, large as life and twice as ugly were four key finder fobs… with not one key on any of them.

Inner demon rolled her eyes but said nothing. I think we are all realising that whatever dad does, he's not trying to be awkward or hard work. He will have put all the key finder fobs away as he won't have remembered what they were for. They would have looked unfamiliar to him, so he has taken them off his keys. Which effectively renders them completely useless.

With still no sign of the missing money, I turned to my sister and said, "We're going to have to have a serious conversation with dad soon."

"I know" she replied "he can't go on living like this. He's not safe".

I think as a family, we've all known that eventually we will have to have dad looked after in a home, but we all know how stubborn and independent he is. Ideally, we all wanted him to stay in his own for as long as possible, but he's becoming a liability to himself.

What if someone down the road really is coming into the house? What if it's not dad's Alzheimer's that's losing money, and he's given it to someone? We know that he paid a fortune to some cowboy not so long ago, to have his drive painted. He's old, and he's vulnerable. All it would take is for someone to realise that he's living alone and not locking the doors, and he's an easy target.

It was there that we made an agonising decision. "We're going to have to look at homes for him." I said. "Yes," my sister agreed. "But it has to be the right one for him." She continued, "Nowhere that's old and smells like cabbages."

"Agreed" I replied.

A while back, after a stay in hospital with his bad knee, we had to book him in to a care home in town for a week's respite, as he was still a bit unsteady on his feet, and not safe to go home just yet. The care home was immaculate, the staff were lovely, but he didn't fit there. The other residents had further advanced dementia than dad, so he had no stimulation. Dad needs to be somewhere that will bring him on, not let him slowly fade away. He needs somewhere that will ignite that spark that's still there sometimes, and not just let him vegetate in a chair.

Back at my sister's house, over a cuppa, we began to search the internet. For when the time came, and we knew it wouldn't be a long way off, we needed to have the right care home in mind. It needed to be near enough that we could visit easily and fit around all of his needs.

At one point we'd investigated the Chelsea Pensioners as in his younger day's dad had mentioned he could be one when he was old. My brother had visited the Royal Hospital with dad for a look around, and my sister and I had spent an entire morning completing the forms. He was turned down on the basis that he had too much help and support at home. Looking back, sending him off to London to live was out of the question.

One of the care homes was literally across the road from me. Ideal location, but after a cursory visit the interior looked dated, and residents had to share bathrooms. If dad's going to move anywhere at his time of life, he needs a bit of luxury around him.

Next search threw up a home in the next village, which I'd heard of as my neighbour works there. The pictures looked amazing, so we decided to go and have a look around. A quick phone call later, and we were heading off to view the home. Pulling into the car park, first impressions were good. The place looked clean and well presented, and we were greeted cheerfully by the lady who we'd spoken to on the phone, who was to show us around. We were heartened by the number of facilities on offer. Ensuite large, modern rooms, a shop, a vintage kitchen, large, well-kept gardens, a cinema and even a pub. They offered activities morning and afternoon, including trips out, live entertainment and singalongs. We knew that dad would be resistant to moving, but if it came to a point where he had to, this place would cater for everything he needed. Some of the residents were Forces Veterans too, which was the icing on the cake.

Feeling slightly relieved that we had some sort of plan mapped out for the future, we messaged our family to tell them the news. The general feeling was sadness, tinged with the realisation that we all knew this would have to happen one day.

Our younger brother in Scotland pinged back some pictures of the holiday, and one was of Mary and dad whizzing along a country road on their mobility scooters. For a while, my brother has been encouraging dad to use the scooter more, but I have to admit, my sister and I haven't been so keen. We have no clue how to use the scooter, and if anything goes wrong with it, or if he went out on it and lost it, we would be the ones who would have to go looking for it.

Looking at the photo, inner demon piped up, "Great! Absolutely marvellous!" She continued, "It's all shits and giggles until he has a crash, gets lost or gets picked up on the dual carriageway thinking he's got a new car!"

Looking at my sister, I said, "This isn't going to go well. He'll be whizzing around on it when he gets back, and we'll never know where he is!". "I know," she agreed. "and it's going to make the care home conversation even more difficult, as he's had a week away with no items to lose, and everything being done for him. He'll have forgotten what it's like day to day and living alone."

Deciding to park the care home idea for a while, as it's blatantly obvious that dad's a bit more compus mentus than we gave him credit for, we awaited dad's return from his holiday. After dropping dad off and settling him in, our brother called me. After commenting on what a great time it looked like they'd had, I gave him a quick overview of our visit to the home, and how it would appear that we'd jumped the gun a bit. He replied, "He'll be ready to go soon, so don't shelve it."

It soon transpired that yes, they had had a lovely time in Scotland, but dad is very reliant on care around him, and not able to spend time alone. He was getting up in the middle of the night and unpacking and re-packing his bags and was forever losing things whilst there as well.

With the plan back in the pipeline, we kept the booked assessment visit.

Knowing dad was safely back from his jollies, I popped down to visit him with some bread. The freezer was full, but I knew he'd need fresh bread and milk. As he opened the door, I noticed he was quite whiskery, when he's always prided himself on having a close shave.

"Where's your razor?" I asked.

He looked confused for a moment whilst he considered that question, then a thought popped back into his head. His eyes lit up with clarity. He jabbed his finger in the direction of outside. "That man – that man down the road came. He took it."

I was pretty sure that the man down the road had little to zero interest in dad's razor. More likely, I thought, that it had been left in Scotland or got mixed up in the packing. There was no point at all in offering this logical explanation, so instead I said, "I'll nip upstairs and have a look for you."

Lo and behold, a quick scout around dad's bedroom revealed the shaver, which was there, in its usual place, but was as flat as a fart as there was no accompanying charger.

Inner demon rolled her eyes and announced, "Great. It could be Absolutely Anywhere!"

Not being able to face a marathon hunt round the house for it, I said brightly, "The shaver's there, but not the charger. It's probably in Charles' car or something." I continued, "I'll nip out and get you a new one – back in 10 minutes." Quickly whizzing up to the supermarket, I bought a new shaver and duly took it back. We plugged it in upstairs, and I moved the old one out of sight so as not to confuse him. Looking pleased that he could have a shave, dad switched it on, then stretched the wire across to the mirror which was slightly too far away to reach comfortably. The mirror obviously has had the ability to angle at some point in its life but has gone loose so it's always pointing down. There he is, one hand on the mirror to keep it still, and the shaver wire stretched to the max, trying to have a shave.

"That doesn't look ideal, dad."

"I know", he nodded.

A picture is hung on the wall directly above where the shaver is plugged in. In his room there are many pictures on the walls, ranging from Army regiment group photos, family photos and some other random pictures. Pointing to the picture nearest to where the shaver charger was plugged in, I said, "Why don't we swap this for a mirror, and then you'll be sorted. A quick scout round in the back bedroom, I spotted a mirror on the wall which would be perfect for the job in hand. Whipping it off the wall, and feeling rather smug with my solution, I took the picture down and hung the mirror in its place. The smug feeling soon dissolved when it became obvious that the mirror was slightly on the large size and wouldn't fit in the gap without pushing the large portrait next to it over to one side.

"We'll have to take this other picture down for now, so it fits" I said.

Pointing at the picture, he says, "That's my grandad". The picture is a large, old family portrait of his grandparents and my grandfather as a child. The pose is formal, and my great grandfather looks quite a formidable character.

Pointing to the small boy on the picture, I said, "Yes, that's right. That's your dad too, isn't it?"

He smiled as if lost in some memory or other.

I continued, "We'll have to put grandad in the other room for now, until we can find a smaller mirror. Is that OK dad?". I took the portrait into the back room and hung it in the spot the mirror used to hang.

Appearing happy with that, he continued his shave in the new mirror.

Inner demon piped up, "You do know it will be all changed back next time you visit?"

"Shh" I replied.

*4 In the Paras*

Dad's back door had been playing up for a while. Either it was stuck shut so he couldn't open it, or it wasn't latching so he was securing it shut with cable ties.

I arranged for chap from a local window company to come down and take a look at it. On arrival at dad's house to let the window man in, I noted that the back gate was wide open, and the front door was unlocked.

When the man arrived, I showed him to the kitchen where the offending door was, and he said that the door just needed a small adjustment, which he could do right there and then.

Leaving him in the kitchen, busy fixing the door, I sat with dad in the lounge. He's got a couple of digital photo frames which we've loaded up with literally thousands of his old photos, right from childhood to his Army days, to family holidays and get togethers.

Calling them the 'Ticker Frames', dad can sit for ages just watching the photographs flick round.

One popped up that I remember being taken in grandma's garden, with all our cousins and aunts and uncles together.

Pointing to the picture, he slowly said, "That's your mam".

"Yes, it is," I reply.

"She was a good one," he smiled wistfully as though remembering the past.

"She certainly was," I smiled back.

My mam died after a short battle with breast cancer back in 1978, when I was nine years old, less than a year after we moved into our new house. I remember dad and my brothers and sister all visiting her in hospital on a Sunday afternoon. The very next day she passed away. His grief at that time must have been incomprehensible. I can't imagine how you would cope with suddenly becoming a widower with four children aged only 43. I do know that he kept everything together for the sake of us all and life carried on. I also know that he threw all the photographs away of that period of our lives which is why my brother digitised all his remaining photographs, to be preserved for future generations.

I remember dad telling me that while mam was in hospital, he had met with her consultant, informing him that he could now take mam home. He'd organised time off work to look after her, and we could all care for her. Holding back his tears he told me the consultant's response.

"I'm sorry, Mr Hoult. You don't understand. Your wife isn't going home."

Dad was obviously recalling this, and his eyes teared up. Searching for the words, he said, "She asked me to get her bed moved – said that everyone in that part disappeared." He went on, "The next day, she died. She knew, you know." Remembering more, he said, "If I had known, I would have taken her home before."

As though he'd realised some ground-breaking information he confidently continued, "Same as my mam… AND my dad… went to hospital and then they died."

As this was the most I've heard him speak in quite a while, I settled back in the chair to allow him to tell his story.

A look of realisation passed through his face, and he said, "Hospitals. That's it. You go in, and you don't come out. They give you a pill and you die." A solid nod of his head confirmed that this was the absolute truth, and he firmly believed every word.

Inner demon's head snapped up and she snorted, "What? I've heard it all now!"

I replied softly, "Mam, Grandma and Grandpa were ill. They were in hospital because they were poorly – nobody gave them a pill."

Dad's convinced now and has warmed to his theme. Nodding quickly, "Yes… yes they do." He said determinedly.

I went on, "Dad, you remember when you went into hospital because of your bad knee?"

A moment of thought, a shake of his head, and "No, I haven't been in hospital".

"You did, dad, and we came to visit. Your knee was all swelled up".

Patting his knee, he looks like he might vaguely remember this. "It still is", he says.

"Yes, we went to the doctor and there's nothing wrong with your knee now, just that it's getting old". I laughed, "And jumping out of planes might not have done it all that much good!" I continued, "Well when you went to hospital because of your knee, you came out. Nobody slipped you a pill, did they?"

He looks unconvinced, thinks for a bit, then replies "No, because I wasn't in the right bed!"

Now on the subject of hospitals, he suddenly remembers a time at least 20 years previously when he was admitted to hospital. After an episode with gout, he used to take pills to prevent this recurring in his earlier days. In their wisdom, his doctor changed the brand which totally disagreed with him and messed up his white blood cell count.

"Yes, I did go to hospital" he states. Seeming proud of himself he continued, "But I didn't want to stay there so I got out!"

I remembered this well. By 'got out' he didn't mean he discharged himself, or that the medical staff thought he was well enough to go home. What actually happened is that he escaped off down the fire escape and went to the pub for a pint.

As if this strengthened the argument, he finished with a triumphant look in his eye, "hospitals… they kill you."

At this, the man busily fixing the door popped his head into the lounge and announced that the door was all fixed. Thanking him, I asked what the bill would be.

Waving me aside, he said, "Nothing, I'll put it down as a service call."

Thanking him and letting him out of the front door, I turned to dad, smiled and said, "Well, that NEVER happens!"

Leaving dad's, I reminded him to lock the door behind me, so that he was safe inside.

5 *Mam and Dad - off to the Mess do*

A couple of days after this, a message pinged in on the carer's Whatsapp group.

"George needs bread and jam please". Reading it, inner demon rolled her eyes, "It's like bloody Groundhog Day", she muttered under her breath.

Realising I wouldn't have chance to nip down today, I texted my sister, as she lives slightly nearer. "Could you pop dad a loaf in please, and I'll add jam to the list next week."

Soon after came her reply "Yes, sure xx".

Another message from the carers, "Had to wake George up to remind him to lock the door after me, sorry!".

Inner demon groaned inwardly.

Later that day, my sister called to tell me she'd dropped the bread in for dad. She then went on to say that she'd found a meal in the microwave, age unknown. He'd insisted it was still OK to eat, point blank refused to let her throw it away and said it wouldn't make him ill. Meanwhile, he was sitting in the lounge eating a pile of biscuits and a slice of bread and butter. We both agreed again that he couldn't continue as he was; he just wasn't safe and looked after properly now at home.

And really at his time of life, he's got to be worth more than a plate of biscuits for his tea.

In moments of optimism, it's crossed both our minds he could come and live with one of us, but in our moments of clarity, we both realised that this just wouldn't work. He's getting more child-like and reliant (but still stubborn!) by the day, and we'd probably end up looking for him in the middle of the night because he'd wandered off to the pub or he'd end up going back to his old house. It confused him enough one time I brought him to my house for the afternoon. He didn't understand I had to take work calls in the back room and thought that I had disappeared on him. On returning to the front room, he was agitated and fretful.

We also must accept the sad reality that he has an illness with no cure and is only going to get steadily worse, and never better.

The time had come to finally make the agonising decision that keeps on rearing its ugly head, and to find alternative accommodation for him, where he would be safe and looked after. We knew in our hearts he would hate this idea, as he has always been fiercely independent and done whatever he wanted, whenever he wanted. There were times in the past where we literally had no idea where he was for months at a time, as he and Mary had gone off touring in the motorhome. Forever with a zest for exploring he definitely preferred the freedom of driving to places himself, and often joked that he'd jumped out of more aeroplanes than he had landed in. He also prided himself on having a great sense of direction, to the point that if you were making a journey, he'd tell you the exact route to take, down to the specific exits off the roundabouts.

He would see leaving his house as a serious clipping of the proverbial wings.

Now, if you've read this far, firstly congratulations for sticking with us, and secondly, you might be thinking, "Hang on a minute! The chap's only lost a few keys and his wallet a few times. Surely there are ways of keeping him safe at home!" Believe me, we had gone through every option, even considered moving someone in with him for full time care. By this stage, he wouldn't understand this concept at all; he'd be packing their bags and evicting them in no time at all.

And it wasn't just a case of leaving doors open and losing things.

We remembered the time my sister had popped in to take some shopping in, and found him confused and withdrawn, sitting in the armchair in the lounge. Slurring his words, he told her that he'd slipped on the ice and his head and neck hurt. But for the life of him couldn't say where or when this had happened. She managed to establish he'd slept in the armchair all night as walking was painful, and he couldn't manage to get up the stairs. Sitting alone in his chair, in pain all night – or could have been even longer must have been so frightening. Calling an ambulance, she explained the situation and was informed that it would be with them in around two hours. Knowing that dad needed medical attention, and two hours was way too long (being 9pm already), she and her eldest son managed to get dad into the car and took him to hospital themselves.

Hours went by as they waited to be seen, and dad asked what time it was.

"12 o'clock" replied my sister.

"Is it dinner time?" he asked.

Dad seriously did not have a clue if it was even day or night.

Noticing dad was becoming increasingly fidgety and tired, my sister hunted out some staff and explained to them that dad most likely had concussion as he was disorientated, and his speech was slurred. They found him a bed and made him more comfortable, the whole time he held tightly on to my sister's hand as he was bewildered and frightened.

Running some tests, dad had an ECG scan which he passed with flying colours. For a man in his eighties, his heart and body were still strong. He also had a CT scan which confirmed that the Alzheimer's was slowly but surely progressing and taking hold, and his brain was deteriorating.

An Xray confirmed that no bones were broken, and dad was discharged.

At 7am the next morning, my phone rang. It was my sister. And she sounded utterly drained and exhausted.

Briefly explaining that she and her son had spent all night in hospital, she wearily asked if I'd come down to sit with dad as they seriously needed some sleep.

"I'm on my way" I replied. "I'll bring McDonald's – you are probably all starving!"

And what about the time where he'd had a fall. Again, he couldn't say when or where he had tumbled, just that his knee was painful and swollen. The story changed each time he tried to tell you; he'd fallen in the pub; he'd fallen in town; a friend had taken him to their house, and he had slept there for the night. He really didn't know what had happened. Into hospital he went for a couple of nights while they drained his knee and kept an eye on him. My sister had popped quickly into his house to pack him an overnight bag. The next day when we visited, we were appalled to see that his pyjamas had obviously not been washed in ages and he looked like a tramp in the bed. Yes, he had carers calling in to do his washing, but they wouldn't think to hunt around for his dirty clothes. He had evidently been putting them away each night in a safe place.

And how about the time that he had turned up at my house on a cold winter's night? He loved to have a wander to pub and would often call at our house first. This winter's night after taking his thin coat from him, we were horrified to discover that he literally only had a vest on underneath and had to wear one of my husband's tops to go home in.

And the time he turned up to Remembrance Parade a full week early in full uniform, or the time he met us at a parade with a huge abscess in his gum that obviously needed treatment.

And when we took him to my uncle's funeral. Despite knowing my uncle since they were teenagers, dad had no idea why he was there and no idea who any of the people there were, even though they were all life-long friends and relatives. He thought he was on a jolly old day out with cake and sandwiches thrown in.

The list of things building up to this moment went on and on. Maybe we had been in denial as to how fast he was deteriorating. Or maybe he was really good at hiding it.

It was now time to seriously start looking for a care home.

It was also now time for us to have this momentous conversation with dad.

We re-booked a home visit from the local care home but arrived at his house beforehand so that we could mentally prepare him as best we could.

On the day, we were a little nervous to say the least. How was this conversation going to pan out? Would he be receptive to more care, or would he put his stubborn foot down, and point-blank refuse any other options? He's often told us firmly in the past, "This is my house", so we were fully aware that this could be a difficult conversation.

Knocking on the door we were happy to notice that this was locked. Dad ambled to the door, opened it, and ushered us in. The first thing he did was rub his knees.

"Are they playing you up again?" my sister asked.

"Yes", he frowned. "Been going to the park – keep moving".

"Do we need a doctor's appointment?" she turned to me.

"We've been twice" I replied. "They say it's just old age. Unless his knees are hot and swollen, it's just a sign of old knees."

I turned to dad and delivered the age-old line, "Maybe jumping out of aeroplanes when you were in the Paras hasn't helped them much!"

At this he nodded and smiled.

We then went on to the task in hand, to broach the subject of more care before the lady from the care home came to assess him.

We reminded him how he frequently lost his keys, and his wallet, and stressed how much we were worried about him being alone now, and that all we wanted for him was to be healthy, safe and looked after. We mentioned his knees and suggested that maybe if he lived somewhere with no stairs, his knees might get a little easier. To our surprise, he seemed fairly open to the idea, so we told him a lady was coming to ask him a few questions, as we'd found him somewhere to try out, to see if he liked it. Somewhere where he'd have all his meals cooked for him and not have to microwave his own; somewhere where there were people he could talk to; entertainment and singalongs, and even a cinema. I think he knows deep down his present life isn't the best it could be, so he agreed that it might be an idea to try somewhere else out. My sister and looked at each other, slightly stunned that it seemed to have gone quite well.

The lady from the care home arrived.

She sat down and began to ask lots of questions – favourite foods, what he like to do, wet or dry shave, lights on or off – we were impressed how thorough the care plan appeared to be. We informed her that I took him to the Veterans' coffee morning once a month and would still collect him for that.

We said that dad played the trumpet and had played in the village band from when he was a young boy.

"Solo trumpet!" dad announced proudly. With that, he reached over and took his trumpet out of the case, blew down the mouthpiece to clean the valves and began to play it. Slightly out of practice, the notes weren't as crisp as they once had been, but it was a tune, nonetheless.

"Need to play every day", dad said.

"Of course, dad", I replied, "bit of practice and you'll soon have it back."

Truth be told, dad has struggled a little with the notes since he had his dentures fitted, as the mouth shape is a bit different to get round the mouthpiece. But, with a bit of practice, I was sure he could still gain some enjoyment from playing.

"Oh, that's lovely," the lady from the care home said. "Reg plays the keyboard, so you can maybe play together!"

Dad seemed pleased with that response. We mentioned again we were going to arrange for him to try to live somewhere else for a little while, but if he didn't like it, we'd find a plan B. Quite what plan B might be, we had not the foggiest, but we could deal with that minor detail if and when we needed to.

To which, dad announced "This is my house".

My sister and I looked at each other and our hearts sank. We knew what we were both thinking. This could be crunch time. This could be the moment where his stubbornness would kick in and he'd demand to stay at home.

"Yes", we agreed. This is your house, and always will be your house. We just want you to try somewhere else to live for a little while, to see if you like it.

"Who will look after the house?" he asked.

"We will." We replied. "We will pop by and make sure it's all looked after and locked up".

Dad seemed happy with that answer, and we breathed a collective sigh of relief.

Later that evening, my sister called and said the care home had been in touch, and had a couple of rooms free, and could take dad any time we wanted.

I agreed to pop over the next day to have a look at the room choices.

Arriving at the care home, I buzzed the door to be let in.

"Hi" I said, cheerily "I've come to have a look at the rooms available for my dad."

"Oh yes", the receptionist replied. She went into the office behind and muttered to someone out of sight, "Which rooms do I show for George?".

Reappearing with a key, she gestured to follow her, and off we went upstairs to look at the rooms.

All the rooms are mainly the same, looking out onto a corridor, and having ensuite wet rooms. It was more the location of the room I was interested in, as we didn't want dad to be stuck up a corridor, out of the way of everything that might be going on. She unlocked the room, and I had a cursory look around. A bit of garden outside to look out on, and the room itself was in between the cinema and the pub, so ideal in that sense.

"It looks OK," I remarked, "What others do you have?"

Looking a tad awkward, she replied, "The manager said to show you this one".

"Oh, we were under the impression there were a couple of rooms to choose from", I replied.

"Not to worry, this looks fine, as it's near to all the things that dad would enjoy". With that, we made our way back downstairs.

Arriving back at reception the manager of the care home was there to greet us.

She was very business-like, and crisply told me the price of the room, payable four weeks in advance on the day of admission. She then went on to say that he could move in any time, preferably within seven days of the assessment.

I remarked it was a massive decision to have to make, which couldn't be made lightly, and it was only now because we felt that he wasn't entirely safe living alone.

To that, she replied "Yes, quite", turned on her heel and returned to her office, leaving me looking slightly awkward in reception.

"Err… I'll call to let you know what's happening next", I said to the lady who'd shown me around.

Climbing into my car, I rang my sister.

"How'd it go?" she asked.

"A bit odd if I'm honest. For a start, there was only one room to look at, and I got the impression they just wanted him in," I told her what had happened, and continued, "I just have a funny feeling about it all. It could be because it's a massive decision, but it needs to be the right decision – not for us, for dad."

"I've had the same feeling", she replied. "I feel like we're being rushed, and I'm really not sure about it."

We recalled what had happened when making the actual care home assessment visit. I had to rearrange the time a couple of times, to fit around my sister's work patterns, and I distinctly heard someone in the background say, "She's changing it AGAIN?". Something was definitely not sitting right with both of us.

"Tell you what", I continued. I'm going to pop into the home that he went to respite in, and just see what they have to offer. At least we will then know that whatever happens, we've covered all options, and explored all avenues."

"Sounds like a plan", said my sister.

Arriving at the second care home, I again buzzed the door to be allowed in. Dad had stayed here briefly before. He'd been on the dementia floor, and although it was only for a week, we didn't feel that the floor met his needs. Dad needs to be brought on, and is very sociable, and some of the residents on the floor really didn't have much to say, due to their illness. The home itself is lovely. Modern, clean, lovely staff and right at the bottom of the road that dad used to live in as a child – so he was super familiar with the area.

A lady let me in, and I asked if it was possible to have a quick chat with someone about possible vacancies. I took a seat, and the manager came out of his office to speak to me. This experience was a million miles away from where I'd just left. A smart looking man approached me, and I explained about our dad, his situation, and how we felt that the time was nearing that he'd need more looking after. I mentioned that dad had been here for short visit a while back, to which the manager replied, "Yes, I remember him! We'll have all his details then and can just add to them."

A lady then popped her head around the door, spotted me and I recognised her as dad's actual next-door neighbour.

I continued to tell the manager that although dad had Alzheimer's, there was still a spark there, and we were looking at homes more to keep him safe and not because he needed round the clock nursing.

Dad's neighbour chipped in, "Yes, I agree. I see George on the front, and he's often confused about things like what day is bin day. He's just slowing down a bit, and just seems a bit lost sometimes."

The manager turned to her, and asked, "Do you think he'd be OK on the ground floor?". Explaining to me, he added "The ground floor is residential, not dementia."

"Yes, certainly." She replied.

This was music to my ears. For dad to potentially be living with the residential people, would mean that he would get the best stimulation, and be able to have conversations and interactions with people who hadn't got advanced dementia.

"We have two rooms" continued the manager, shall we arrange an assessment?

"Brilliant", I smiled. How about half 4 on Thursday? I went for half 4 in case my sister wanted to come along too, so she'd be able to arrange to leave work a bit earlier.

"Marvellous" said the manager. "I'll see you then!"

My heart felt much lighter on leaving the home, and I instantly called my sister to update her. Collectively our feeling was much more positive about this place from the building, the location, the staff and the choice of rooms here.

"I'll call him to nail down these rooms", she announced. "We don't want them falling through!"

Later that evening, she called me again (I honestly don't think I've spoken so much to my sister in my whole life!).

"Good news", she announced. "They have two rooms available on the ground floor. One overlooking the walkway, and one overlooking the park. Both will be available after the assessment on Thursday".

We agreed that after the assessment, we'd take dad to have a look at the rooms and see which he preferred. At this point, it's still for a few weeks, and it has to be his choice if he stays forever. But we're hoping that he likes it so much that he wants to stay. We hope he will enjoy having hot meals prepared, activities, company and stimulation, that he'll think it's a good idea. We personally think that it's got to be better than living alone, shuffling around the park and living on microwave meals and plates of custard creams.

Thursday came, and I drove down to dad's house for the assessment. When he let me in, I made small talk, then told him that someone was coming to see him to ask a couple of questions. A short while later, a knock at the door signalled that Paul the manager of the care home had arrived. I answered and welcomed him into the living room. I've noticed that although dad's house is clean and tidy, it smells a bit old and fusty at times. Is this something that just happens? Do houses get old inside, in time with their occupants?

Paul sat down opposite dad and whipped out his paperwork. "Now, George" he boomed. "Just going to go through a couple of things, to see if anything has changed since the last time we saw you. Does that sound OK?"

"Yes" replied dad.

Paul then went through what medication dad was on, eating habits, preferences etc – no change. He then mentioned his memory, and I told him that dad was getting steadily more forgetful but could remember things from long ago. I added that we, as a family didn't feel confident about dad living alone for much longer, as he tends to lose keys and not lock doors. Happy that he had all the answers he needed, Paul then stood up to shake dad's hand. Looking up at Paul, towering above him, dad remarked "You're a big lad!". We all laughed.

"Tell you what," said Paul, "Why don't you come for lunch tomorrow? See how you like us? We've got a singer on".

"That sounds like a lovely idea" I replied. We arranged to visit around 11 o'clock the next morning, and I wrote it on dad's big desk calendar.

The morning after, I whizzed down to dad's house to find him clean and tidy, and ready to go. He seemed excited to be going out, which was a great start, and proudly informed me that he'd had a shower.

We got into the car and I drove to the care home. The home is at the bottom of the street where he was born, so I made a conscious decision to drive down that road to get there, so he felt like he was in familiar territory. We entered the home and were shown into the lounge. All the residents were gathered there for the singer to begin, and we took our seats near the back of the room.

The singer began his act, and I have to say, he was brilliant. He sang a good mix of songs, and his flirting skills with the old dears was priceless. They loved him! The staff made every effort to involve the residents, getting them to sing along, and everyone was having a grand old time. I had a feeling from deep within, that dad would be more than alright here. One of the staff was having a dance with one of the men, and I clocked dad tapping his feet.

"Do you want to dance, dad?" I asked. "I'll have a dance with you".

He nodded and manoeuvred himself out of the chair. Making our way to the empty space at the front of the room, we weaved in and out of the seated residents. Squeezing past one of the chaps, I felt his hands either side of my waist as he copped a cheeky feel. As we passed, I could hear him giggling to himself.

Taking our place, we began to dance. Dad was a bit of a charmer on the dance floor back in the day, and the old jive movements were soon coming back to him. He remembered to lead me in the twirls and twists, and I could tell he was enjoying himself immensely. After a good few songs (and a round of applause), we returned to our seats. After the singer had ended his set, Paul the manager came over and showed us to a quiet lounge where our table was set for lunch. On the way there, we passed the cinema, which we popped our heads in for a look. The place was amazing – a big screen, with comfortable seats laid out in cinema style – there was even a popcorn machine.

Sitting down for lunch, we were served sandwiches, crisps and cakes, and a can of beer for dad. I eased us into the topic of staying for a while, saying that we were all getting worried about him living by himself, as we didn't think he was safe. I told him that we worried if he'd locked the doors, and worried that he was lonely, and worried that he wasn't eating properly. At this he looked sad.

I explained that it wasn't *him* that forgot to lock up and eat, it was just his memory. It wasn't his fault, and he hadn't done anything wrong; his mind just forgot things nowadays. He digested this for a while and slowly nodded, seeming a bit happier with that. I suggested that he could come and stay here for a bit, as there were no stairs and hopefully it would ease some of the pain he had in his knees. He looked around, assessing the place and said, "Stay here?".

"Yes, dad – just for a while to see if you like it. You'll have lovely food, singers and entertainment, and lots going on for you to join in with. What do you think? Fancy a try?"

"How much… how much does it cost?"

Now, I know full well that if I mention it's £1000 a week, there's no way on earth he'll want to try it. "Don't you worry about that," I replied, "We'll sort it all out for you." At this point, I think dad has promoted the magic fairy status that I have. Not only do I buy all his shopping, but I'm also now paying all his bills!

*Spoiler alert – we have Power of Attorney, so it comes out of his accounts eventually. Yes, the care home is expensive, but it's seriously on par with a top hotel. Dad has worked hard and saved hard for his money, and really, we'd prefer that he lived out the rest of his life in luxury, rather than scrimping and leaving it all to us.

Seeming happy with that, he agreed to try staying here for a couple of weeks.

Paul then returned and proceeded to show us the available two rooms. The first was the show room, which was immaculately decorated and overlooked the park. Shuffling to the window, dad said something we couldn't quite understand, but it was about the park.

"Yes, dad" I replied – it's the park you used to play on as a kid.

He pointed to the right and said something else that we didn't quite get.

"That's right, the swings used to be over that side, but they've moved them to just here now."

He smiled and nodded.

The second room was up the corridor and overlooked the car park. There really was no comparison. The first room would be ideal. I told Paul our decision, and he asked when dad wanted to come. Deciding to strike whilst the iron was hot, and whilst the 'trying out' conversation might stay in dad's memory, I replied that we would be back the next day. I figured if we left it a week, we would have the whole discussion to go through again, as dad simply wouldn't remember it.

I agreed with Paul that dad would come for a couple of weeks, then we could take it from there. He added that if dad did end up staying, his room could be made his own, and the maintenance man would put up any pictures for him. He could also bring in small items of furniture from home.

Leaving the care home and arriving at dad's house, I wrote on his calendar that my sister and I would pick him up the next day. Later on, I called my sister, and we were both so very pleased with how it had all gone. I mentioned to her that dad had said something about 'putting a ticker on his house', which I assumed was a For Sale board, which we took with a pinch of salt at this stage, as dad can still change his mind like the wind, when old Mr Stubborn pops into his head. We arranged to meet up the next morning.

Surprisingly when we arrived, dad did seem to have remembered where he was going. We told him that we'd pack a little bag for him and take some of his photos in too. He could also take his trumpet in, so he could play some tunes while he was there. I went off upstairs to pack some clothes and hunted about for a small suitcase that I knew was up there somewhere. I finally located it in the bottom of a wardrobe, pulled it out and realised it was full.

Inner demon groaned. What's going to be inside that? Every day's an adventure, she rolled her eyes.

Placing it on the bed, I opened it. It was full of clothes, and right in the middle of these was his shaver charger that 'the man up the road had stolen'.

This was obviously the case that had gone to Scotland with him that he'd forgotten to unpack. Not knowing which were clean or dirty, I piled them all in a bag to take home to wash.

Filling the case back up with a few essentials for his stay, I returned downstairs and told dad and my sister that the shaver charger had turned up. She meanwhile had done a grand job of collecting a few personal belongings together, such as photos and his calendar and clock so he had some familiar things around him, so we were ready to go.

Arriving back at the care home, we made our way to dad's new room and set about arranging his photos and putting his clothes away. Dad even hung his own clothes up in the wardrobe. Putting some beers and a bottle of whisky in the cupboard and carefully placed his trumpet case under the dressing table. When all was complete, we turned the digital photo frames on and angled them towards the chair at the window so he could see them.

Spotting the trumpet case, he gestured "Have you got the…" and tailed off. "The music, dad? And the stand?". He nodded. "Yes, they're in the cupboard".

Pointing at the trumpet case, he continued "That lad… that lad came and broke it". We knew there was some problem with the trumpet, as he'd shown us earlier that you couldn't blow through it. Not being players ourselves, we had no clue what could be wrong with it but had decided to take it into the home where our brother (who does play) could have a look when he visited.

"No, dad, a lad didn't come and break it, but we know it doesn't work. Charles will have a look when he comes to see you".

He seemed happy with that response, so we all had a cup of tea as we settled him in to the room, and left a while later with him quietly looking out over the park and the garden.

The next couple of months sailed by relatively drama free and life assumed a steady rhythm once more. My sister and I, and our aunt, popped in every couple of days to see that dad was OK and settling in. Some visits we'd have a cup of tea and a chat; on others we'd take him for a little walk in the park. He enjoyed our visits and we enjoyed visiting, because now, they didn't involve searching his house for missing items, and trying to wrestle out of date food out of his fridge and into the bin. I don't think we realised how exhausting it was before, and how drained we all were. Everything seemed calmer, more tranquil, and it was lovely to have quality time with dad. It was as though we all breathed a collective sigh of relief, knowing he was safe, well looked after, and not wandering around town late at night flashing his wallet around. Full of pictures and portraits from his house, his room was really homely, and we'd even arranged for him to have his own little fridge with a regular supply of beer inside. He'd always enjoyed a beer or two in the evening, and this just helped keep some of his routines going.

Dad seemed more content too. He visibly started to gain some weight, clearly enjoying the menu choices on offer. Now he was always clean and tidy, and smartly dressed, clean shaven and his hair combed back 'just so'.

It soon became apparent though that he needed new shoes. The ones we had packed for him were a touch too tight as his feet seemed slightly swollen. My son and I picked dad up for a shoe shopping trip. Parking the car dad walked slowly with us towards the shoe shop in the High Street. They had a sale on, and we figured that we should definitely be able to find something suitable for him to wear. We ambled along, with dad seeming to struggle a little to keep pace. Slowing to accommodate him, eventually we reached the shop. I sat dad down and proceeded to present him with different styles of shoe. We soon realised this might be a tad more challenging than we first thought. Some shoes were too narrow, some he didn't like the style of, some were too formal and so we went on. Eventually I flagged down the services of a friendly shop assistant, and explained we needed extra wide fit in dad's size. He produced a lovely leather pair, with an adjustable Velcro strap across the front. Perfect. Bending down, he placed them gently on dad's feet to see how they fit.

"How do they feel, Sir?"

Dad thought for a while, wriggled his toes and his face broke out into a beaming smile. From this reaction we knew that they were a good fit.

"Can you have a little walk up and down to see if they are comfy?" asked the store assistant.

Dad slowly rose to his feet and gingerly put one foot in front of the other. And then, I absolutely kid you not, to the amusement and entertainment of everyone in the shop, he started to march around the shop. Seeing the reactions of our fellow shoppers, he grinned heartily and broke out into a trot. Not half an hour earlier, he was struggling to walk, and now you'd think he was in training for a half marathon. After a lap of the shop and a small round of applause from everyone, he arrived back to us.

"I take it they are good shoes then dad?" I laughed. "Keep them on, and I'll pay for them."

Looking puzzled, he countered, "How… much?..."

"Nothing to you, dad – these are on me." The magic fairy strikes again!

We then all went to the pub for a breakfast and a pint, after which we took him back to the home knowing he'd had a jolly good trip out.

In the reception area was a notice board with the varied range of activities on offer, including singers, film afternoons, dominoes with the cubs and so on… literally something for everyone.

On arrival, we mentioned to the 'Pink Ladies' – the ones who wore pink tabards and oversaw all the entertainment, how varied the activities were.

"Yes" she replied. There's always lots going on. Your dad likes it when we have the singers in the afternoon."

We agreed that dad had always liked his music.

She laughed, "He's quite a mover, your dad. Everyone can't wait to get him up for a rock and roll!"

So, dad probably wouldn't remember the trip to the shoe shop or what he had for breakfast, but the old moves were still there. He always did love a good dance.

A couple of days later, I arrived at the home to pick dad up for our monthly outing to the Veteran's coffee morning. As usual, I made my way along the corridor to his room, knocked on the door and let myself in.

All was neat and tidy, and dad was sitting in his usual spot, looking out of the window. His room has a lovely outlook, as he can see across to the other side of the park and can also see the primary school children in the playground next door. Quite often the parents picking up their children after school will take a detour to the park, so the sounds of happy children chattering and laughing often makes its way up to his room.

Dad looked smart and clean, I also noticed that he looked better in himself. His cheeks had filled out slightly, and he had clearly put on a few more pounds round the middle. This was a contrast from when he was living at home. He'd slowly been losing weight there, due to him forgetting to warm up his microwave meals or eating an erratic diet. At one point we discovered he was buying a kebab on the way home from the pub and having half that evening and warming the rest up the day after. No, he was certainly looking healthier. I also noticed that he looked calmer. At home, he was forever losing things, patting down his pockets for his missing wallet or keys; or thinking that people were coming into his house. It's hard to put a word on it, but looking at him how, he looks less anxious, and more settled. Less twitchy.

"Are you ready, dad?" I asked. "We're off to the coffee morning".

Looking puzzled, he raised one eyebrow. I continued. "The coffee morning. You know… where we go with the veterans."

Dad furrowed his brow. I continued, "In the place near the car park, by the church."

His eyes widened, with a slight nod of his head, and I knew that he'd placed it.

"Come on then, let's go."

Dad mumbled something that was incoherent and reached for my arm. Holding it firmly, he searched in his mind for the words he needed, looked me deep in the eyes, and slowly said,

"I… can't …stay… here…all… my…life."

If I'm honest, I shouldn't have been surprised and should have anticipated this conversation at some point. Although he seemed quite content, we had caught him lurking around the exits trying to break free. In his mind he probably just fancied a walk out he couldn't go out alone. When he was on the ground floor he'd be hovering around in Reception to work out where the button was for the door, which made the receptionist a little nervous. After a few failed attempts dad was moved up to the top floor being much more secure, needing a code to call the lift up and down. We totally agreed with this decision; after all, if he went missing, they would be responsible for him, and it was their duty to keep him safe and well.

My heart lurched as I searched within myself for my answer. As a family, we always knew that it was never going to be an easy thing for him to live somewhere else, and up to this point, he's probably thought he was on holiday. Now, the determined, strong, independent man inside had bubbled to the surface and was having his say. As a family we have had some agonising conversations about the whole thing, and unanimously agreed that he couldn't ever go back to his house.

I swallowed hard. It's one thing having this conversation with your siblings, but quite another story having to break it to your dad. The man you've looked up to all your life… the man who's been the rock of the family and always made up his own mind and his own decisions. The man who has always been the head of the house, the strong provider, always looking out for us.

Kneeling down beside his chair, I took his hand and met his gaze, pleading silently with him to understand what I was about to say.

"Dad, you know that I love you, don't you? That we all do?"

His eyes confirmed that he did.

"You weren't safe at home, dad. That's why you are staying here. You can't go back to your house."

Dad looked confused, and I nearly lost it. Biting my lip so that I wouldn't cry, I carried on in earnest. "Dad, we love you, and we want you to have a long life, where you are safe, and have nice food, and where you are looked after. We want you to live a long time and be somewhere you are happy. Do you understand?"

I continued, "Your house isn't safe for you anymore. If there was any way we could have let you stay there, we would have found it." My voice cracked as I concluded, "You have to stay here now".

He paused a second, to take this in. Looking around his room, drinking in all his photographs and pictures on his walls from his old house, he then looked at me and slowly and sadly nodded. I knew that at that moment, he realised that he had to stay.

I'd just had the most difficult conversation, I think, of my entire life.

*6 Me as a baby*

A couple of days later, my sister called. During this entire time, I think one of the most positive things to come out of it is the strong bond we've formed. Don't get me wrong, we've always been close, but since we've been responsible for all the 'dad decisions', we've become even closer still. I honestly don't think I could have done it all on my own, and I'm sure she feels the same. We are each other's sounding boards, moaning blocks and generally somebody to scream, "What now!!" at.

Answering the call, before I could speak, she blurted out, "You'll never guess what?"

Not knowing yet whether this was going to be a funny 'guess what' story, or a full-on drama, I replied tentatively, "What?"

"Well," she continued. "Went to see dad this afternoon, and he was a bit whiskery. I asked him if he'd had a shave, and he said someone had come in and taken his shaver out of the bathroom." Pausing for breath, she carried on, "So… I tried to reassure him nobody would come and take anything, and everything in his room was safe.

He was adamant that people came in to take things away, and I kept trying to tell him that they wouldn't steal anything from him.

He didn't look at all convinced, so I said that it must be here, in the room, and started to look through all his cupboards."

"What did you find?" I asked.

"Nothing! Looked in all the drawers, cupboards and everywhere. Couldn't find the shaver anywhere – not one sign of it".

"Did you check the usual shelf? Under his pyjamas?" I asked.

"Everywhere," she replied. Every drawer, every shelf… even in the fridge!" She continued,

"I was just about to go and ask at the desk if they had seen it when he starts faffing around getting his trumpet out. I waited around to see if he was going to play it, and what was in the case?"

"The shaver?" I ventured.

"Yes! The blooming shaver was in his trumpet case! Can't think why I didn't think to look there first!"

"What did he do?"

"He looked at it as if to say, how on earth did the shaver get there, and went back to getting the trumpet out to play. I plugged it all back in the bathroom and told him that nobody had stolen it after all."

We laughed about this latest incident in the drama that was our dad and unanimously agreed nothing ever seemed to be straightforward. We also wondered how on earth he could lose so many things in just one room, and thanked our stars that he no longer had a whole house of a vortex to swallow things up in.

Dad's wife currently lives with her daughter. She moved there a few years ago as her health was suffering, and it became impossible to continue living in the house with dad. Looking back, this was the start of the signs of his Alzheimer's taking hold, but at the time, we all just thought he was being a man whose behaviour was becoming difficult with age. It all came to a head when she had a fall in the house, and dad was unable, or unwilling to call her an ambulance. That experience would have frightened her, as it would anybody, and they realised they couldn't live together in the house. For a start there's no central heating in there, so it's cold in the winter. There's no downstairs toilet, and the stairs are on the steep side.

At first, they looked at buying a house together that was nearer to her daughter. That way, she would have the security of knowing her family was nearby, but they could also live in a more modern house. They did view a few houses, but none came up to scratch. Dad was never keen, not wanting to leave his hometown, so from the beginning, they were in a bit of a catch 22 situation – he was never going to like any of them. After a lot of thought and discussion, they decided that dad would stay in the house, and Mary would move in with her daughter. Not entirely ideal, and not entirely traditional, but I remember when they told us of their plans, they just wanted the best for Mary's health. He even said something along the lines of he'd lost two wives already, and he wasn't about to lose a third. And it wasn't as though they weren't still happily married. They were. They still went on trips together, met up for lunch and had a wander around the shops. They still loved each other and enjoyed being together. They still spoke often on the telephone. Just lived in different houses.

Since being with her family, Mary's health has improved dramatically, and she always looks well and healthy, so the right decision was made for all the right reasons.

On a recent phone call with her, she mentioned that she would like to come and visit dad, and we arranged that I'd meet her and her daughter at the home, to show them around and which room dad was in. We duly met up, and I gave them the whistle stop tour of the place; the cinema room, the common living rooms and the quiet lounges that people could use. They both seemed relieved and impressed that dad was living in such a lovely place. Reaching dad's floor, we spotted him sitting with the gents, eating his lunch, so I led them off to his room so they could see that first. We'd only just reached it, when dad came ambling up behind us – he must have clocked us walking past, which had to be a good thing, as he'd obviously recognised us.

Then followed a conversation about the room, and how nice the home was. We looked at the photos all around and he struggles to put names to all his children, but he knows for definite that the black and white portrait is of his grandad. All signs of the disease, as the more distant memories are remembered for longer. All signs that one day, my name and the names of my brothers and sisters would gradually slip away from his mind. But for now, he knows our faces and knows we belong to him; just struggles with what we're all called.

Dad went quiet, as though he was searching for some words, and I kind of knew what was coming next.

"If I go up that road," he gestured towards the front of the building. "If I go up that road, and…" his hand pointed right, "I can go to the house".

He was describing how to get to his old house.

"Dad," I replied calmly. "You don't live there anymore. You live here. You can't live in that house, as there are stairs, and your knees don't like stairs. You are safe here, and we know that you are looked after. Do you remember?"

He pondered this information for a second or two and furrowed his brow.

Mary then added, "Yes George. You live here now. This is your home. And you're really lucky to have such a lovely place to live."

He thought a bit more and seemed to take this on board. For now.

Diverting the topic of conversation, I'd noticed that there was a singer booked on the ground floor, so asked Mary, her daughter and dad if they'd like to go and have a look. Thinking that that might be a nice end to the visit, we proceeded to the lift and I punched in the access number. Dad has asked my sister and I in the past what the number is, and we tell him a random number each time. The only thing that dad misses whilst living in the home is the freedom to come and go as he pleases. We counterbalance that with the knowledge that he's done whatever he darn well pleased for more than 80 years of his life, so it's not a massive hardship for him. By telling him a random number for the lift, we figure that if he wanted to go out, by the time he'll have got to his room to get his jacket, and back to the lift again, he will have forgotten what the number was. You have to use this illness to your advantage sometimes.

Arriving on the ground floor, there were no signs of the singer, but the lounge was full of residents and one of the pink ladies. I asked if there was a singer on, and she told us that she hadn't turned up yet, and they were having a quiz instead. We took our seats to join in. I can't praise the pink ladies highly enough. They are the ones who organise the activities, and they really engage and involve everyone in whatever they are doing. The quiz was conducted with enthusiasm and humour, and everyone who got a question right got a 'yay!' and a high five. Towards the end of the quiz, we made movements to leave – Mary and her daughter needed to miss the traffic, and I needed to get back to work. Making our way to the reception area, we began to say our goodbyes to dad, and he said, "It's OK, I will see you out".

Inner demon piped up, "Great! You know if he gets out, it will be the devil's job to get him back in again! He'll be OFF!"

Knowing this to be true, and panicking ever so slightly, I scanned around for a member of staff to come and help us, but there was nobody at the desk, and nobody except the pink quiz lady in the lounge around.

Stalling our goodbyes to keep him away from the door, I asked, "Shall I take you back up in the lift?"

"No, I'll come out" was the reply.

"You need to stay in here, dad" I said. "You can't be wandering around out there."

In the nick of time, the pink quiz lady must have spotted us from the lounge, and she approached dad.

"Come and do the quiz with us, George," she boomed, taking hold of his hand.

"We're a man down on the team, and we really need your help!"

At the thought of someone needing his help, dad's chest puffed up ever so slightly, he smiled at us, and allowed himself to be led back into the lounge.

We all looked at each other and let out a collective sigh of relief.

*7 Camping with my older brothers and sister*

With dad safely ensconced in the home (albeit trying to make a run for it on the very odd occasion), the time had come for us to start sorting out his house. It was never going to be an easy task, and it was made so much worse because he was still with us. I think, if somebody dies, then it's a full stop if you like – the house sorting business is inevitable. Because dad is still here, it almost felt like we were invading his personal space.

As a family, we have agreed that we'll get the house updated and rent it out. That way, it's still his property, and the rent will go some way towards the nursing home bills. We have the builders lined up and raring to go. But they can't start the work until the house is empty.

Our younger brother was travelling up with a big trailer, and we'd arranged for the furniture to be donated to a charity that helps people who suddenly find themselves homeless. The furniture was old, but still serviceable, and we felt happier that it would be put to good use and at least help some people who were less fortunate than ourselves.

Our elder brothers and my sister's husband all pitched up too, to help move the heavy stuff and load up the trailer.

Venturing inside the house, my sister and I started on the task of systematically clearing the small stuff room by room. We'd emptied the kitchen cupboards a week or so earlier, and in the process had found a festering meal still in the microwave, age unknown.

We'd also moved all his sentimental objects, such as his medals and jewellery out of the empty house and had photographed and catalogued everything before putting it into safe storage. He himself had made an itemised list of his precious items, together with who he wanted them to go to after he died. We were lucky to find his paperwork all filed away in an orderly fashion too.

Now all that was left to do was to sort out and box up the rest of the house. We both looked at the daunting task ahead of us. The house still smelled of dad, and there were wardrobes and drawers full of clothes he had once worn. Dad was never one to spend money on himself, so there were some clothes that had clearly seen better days, and some that had been returned to the wardrobe time after time and hadn't seen the washing machine in a very long time. We deduced that dad would have worn a shirt and hung it up in the wardrobe at night. The next day he would have returned to the wardrobe and forgotten all about the fact he'd worn the shirt the previous day and put it back on again. Some of the collars of the shirts were brown, so these went straight in the bin. It saddened us to think that although we'd had helpers going in each day, dad would have been wearing dirty, old clothes. The 'old' dad in him would have been mortified too. He always prided himself on looking smart and dapper. My aunt remembered when she was a child, watching him getting ready to go out – suit and tie on, combing back his hair and singing 'Walking my baby back home". We all remember him getting ready to wander to the pub at 9pm sharp. Always in smart trousers, a shirt and tie and a smart blazer.

Looking around the rooms, it became more than obvious that the house had suffered a level of neglect as well. Surfaces hadn't had a proper clean in a while; carpets that could have done with a good hoover round, and the whole place was a bit, well… sticky.

We soon developed a system of things to keep, sentimental stuff, paperwork and the like. Next pile was charity shop, and the last was rubbish. Because of his illness, we found collections of random items, all neatly lined up, with a towel placed on the top. Under one towel was a neat line of watches, another had a line of combs. We concluded that he would have sorted things out, then put a cover over them so nobody could find them. Trouble was, he, himself changed the locations of all the objects, putting things in ever safer places so he couldn't find anything anyway. This was probably where the story about the 'man up the road' came about, who kept coming in and taking things.

At the bottom of one drawer, I came across a little blue notebook, slightly bashed around the edges. Opening it up, I caught my breath, and beckoned my sister over. Inside, was the unmistakable scrawl of our dad's handwriting. It was a diary that he had started to write.

"He knew." I said. "He knew ages ago that he was ill." Looking more closely at the little book, I groaned. "Oh god, he knew a year before his diagnosis."

Look – he's written everything out so that he can go back and remember it." Flicking through the pages, we were filled with a great sadness. The book had started out meticulously labelled with the date in the margin, and what had happened on that day. Just normal everyday things he'd done. Towards the end of the book the handwriting became more erratic, the text more rambling, and the entries more sporadic.

He wrote on one page, *I shall now try to note in this book to help me remember things. Things I have been to*. He wrote about trips to the pub, and to the park, about what he had for dinner, and even about how he made up sentences so he could find his car number plate in the car park. It transpired that on several occasions he had driven to town, returned home to find he'd left his car in town. He then had to go back to try and find where he'd left it. At one point he writes *I know that this is a very poor writing, and I will be better*. He wrote about me picking him up for the Drs appointment and how he hoped they would find out what was wrong with him.

Just before we closed the book, a scrap of paper fluttered out. It has his name and address on it.

We realised with heavy hearts that he'd have carried that around in case he got lost.

With an added sadness that hadn't been there ten minutes earlier, we silently continued with the essential job of clearing his house, we also realised once again that we had made the right decision, the *only* decision. There was no way he could have stayed here. But why do we always feel so damn guilty about it?

Downstairs, our brothers were busy loading up the trailer for the charity. Our elder brother lives a way away, and he agreed to take a box of photos and sentimental items, including some videos, over to Mary on his way home.

After we loaded up his car and busied ourselves with our goodbyes, we mentioned the diary to him, and the continued feeling of guilt we carried around with us.

"He's having a great time." He announced cheerfully.

My sister and I looked at each other and then to him with a "How do you even know?" kind of expression.

He continued, "We watch him on Facebook. He's always on there!"

"Facebook?" I asked, thinking how did we not know about this little gem of information.

"Yes," our brother continued, "the home has a Facebook page. He's dancing around on the videos, and there's one of him playing his trumpet for the Mayor."

"Oh," we replied. "We didn't even know they had that."

After he had left with his car full of stuff to deliver, we whipped out our phones and did a quick search online.

Sure enough, there was the page, complete with photos and videos. Smiling, dancing and playing his trumpet. And looking completely fine, and not hard done to at all. With the dark cloud we carried around lifted slightly, and with a great sense of relief, we continued with the task in hand.

With the house empty, it was time to call in the builders. They had already quoted us for the whole job, which was basically to rip the place apart and start again. All the polystyrene ceiling tiles had to go, and the house needed decorating from top to bottom. A new kitchen and bathroom were to be installed, and as the place had no central heating, we were having the gas connected. Dad always refused to have central heating installed, as he insisted that oil radiators did him just fine. This was all well and good until they started tripping out the electric, and his illness made him forget how to trip it all back on again. It was a happy moment indeed when those radiators went in the skip, as we never did know which was the dodgy one.

*8 Army days*

## Chapter 18 - September 2019

A week or so later I was sitting on the sofa, watching TV and my phone pinged. It was a text from my sister.

Random question, when we cleared the house, did we get rid of all the old pairs of glasses?

I replied – Pretty sure so – why?

Immediately afterwards, my phone rang, and inner demon groaned and said "What on earth can it be now? It's 8 o'clock on a Friday night, and I DO NOT want to be talking about dad's specs!"

Sensible me answers the call.

"Not sure quite what's gone on," my sister said.

"Try me" I answered.

"Weeeellll. The home called and said that they'd done a routine eye test on dad, and he needs new glasses".

"Already?", I countered "He's only just had some".

Inner demon chimed in "We all vividly remember that fun-packed afternoon in the opticians having his eyes tested!"

"I know" my sister continued. "Spoke to the home and apparently the ones he has on are about 10 years old".

"So where are his new ones?"

"Your guess is as good as mine" she replied.

"And how has he got old glasses in there? We only took in his new ones".

Again, she replied, "No idea".

I thought for a second and countered, "Maybe they aren't his? Maybe they are some other poor chaps' who's now wandering around blind as a bat!"

"Could well be," my sister considered this. "Either way, we'll never know for sure".

We decided that we'd have a good look around for his new glasses the next time we visited. Concluding that they probably weren't his, or an old pair had snuck in via a jacket pocket or something. Worst-case scenario we'd just have to order him a replacement pair.

My sister then began to laugh.

"What now?" I ventured

"I forgot to tell you I popped in yesterday. When I left, I went to get him a beer from the fridge, and he'd switched the setting on it to 'hot'. I'm surprised the whole thing didn't explode!" She continued, "I reached in for a can and it was boiling hot with the top popped up. I almost chucked it at him because I couldn't hold it!".

I laughed at this mental image of the beer equivalent of a hot potato.

"Why has the fridge got a hot setting?" I ventured.

"God only knows," she replied. "But why are we not surprised that it has, and he found it!" She continued, "I've asked them to keep an eye on the fridge setting and make sure it's always on 'cold'".

"And there's more", Sharon continued. I went to put his telly on, and he said that he had buggered it up. I switched it on, and he'd only got it stuck on the adult channel, and the remote had frozen!"

Inner demon guffawed, "The adult channel! That's hilarious!".

Nearly spitting out my wine, I said, "The adult channel? What's he doing with that?"

"No idea, but obviously I couldn't go and ask reception. It wasn't on any mucky image or anything, just the name of the channel came up. No idea what's actually on it! I turned it all off and on again, and it seemed to do the trick."

Laughing I asked her, "Do you think the home have subscribed them all to round the clock porn?" I continued, "I've just had a mental image of everyone sloping off for 'an early night'.

"Oh god" she replied, "there are some mental images that just can't be un-seen! Thanks for that!"

Both giggling now, we surmised that this would be a highly unlikely scenario, and a more logical explanation would be a perfectly innocent channel that slipped through on Freeview or something.

"It was lucky that you fixed it then!"

Inner demon pulled a face and said, "How much can go missing, or go wrong with one man, in one room?"

After the call, I turned to her and said, "erm… wrong glasses, missing glasses, boiling hot beer and a frozen TV. Not bad for one day's adventures – all in the one room!" I continued, "I think that's quite an achievement, even by dad's standards".

*9 Dad with my step mum, Pat*

A couple of days later I turned up at the home bright and early, to collect dad for a trip to the Arboretum in Staffordshire. This was a trip organised by Joining Forces and Age UK for the members of the Veterans' coffee mornings. I'd never been before but snaffled a place on the coach trip by default of my volunteering at the group. The bus was leaving at 9am prompt, so I'd called the home in advance to tell them I'd be picking him up early, and could they make sure he was nice and smart, with his new shoes on, and ready to leave at 8.30am. Not being sure if he would have had time to eat breakfast that early, I made him a snack he could have on the coach if needed.

Entering his room, I was delighted to see that yes, he was ready and smart, and by the looks of it had just polished off a full English. He looked vaguely puzzled to see me, and I said "We're off out on a trip today, Dad. You look lovely and smart… are you ready to go?"

His eyes lit up at the mention of a trip out, and he enthusiastically said "Yes!"

Hauling himself out of the chair, he collected up his plate and cup, I took them from him, and we ambled off down the corridor, dropping them off at the dining room en-route. Driving up to the pick-up point, in plenty of time for the trip, I dropped dad off and stood him with my aunt and uncle whilst I parked the car and walked back to them. People soon began to arrive and chatted together whilst waiting for the bus. When it arrived, everyone started to find their places, but some people, including dad, had to embark using the lift as the coach steps were a tad too steep to navigate safely. This was halfway down the bus and was quite ingenious. One half of a door flipped out to reveal a platform that was the lift, and the other half of the door opened to create a space for people to enter the bus once they were level. Once everyone was aboard, after a quick head count, we were on our way.

In no time at all, we'd arrived at the Arboretum, and it was time for everyone to get back off the bus. Dad and I stood in the opening waiting for the lift to come up, and I think he had a flash back of being in the Paras. He made a "sheeew" kind of noise and did an action like he was jumping out of a plane. He was making me nervous being so close to the opening, as together with him being a bit unsteady on his feet, I feared that he might actually chuck himself off the bus. I moved him away a bit until the lift reached us. Once safely on firm terrain, we made our way to reception to hire him a mobility scooter. The Arboretum is a huge place dedicated to honour people who have served our country, such as the armed forces. The place is massive, and really spread out, but there's loads to see. We'd never get around if he were walking.

After filling in the scooter forms, the chap at reception brought out dad's scooter, to give him a quick crash course. Alan from the group had been ahead of us in the queue, so he'd had his course and was on his test drive, whizzing around reception and nearly clearing us up in the process. Dad sat on the scooter, and it looked fairly simple to operate. Button forward for forward, and back for back. The chap pointed to the speed button and said that once dad had got the hang of it, he could make it go a bit faster if he wanted. Once that was all done, we were on our way. Tentatively at first, dad pushed the button forward, and the scooter began to move. His face lit up, as, always a keen driver, it was as though he'd got his wheels back, and he proudly proceeded to do a perfect three-point turn in the square, beaming from ear to ear. So, off we went, my aunt, uncle, dad and I, in search of the Royal Engineers Memorial. Next, we headed for the main memorial on the mount, and dad's confidence was visibly growing by the minute. He was having a grand old time.

"Dad," I said, "You're doing really well on that. Do you want to turn the speed up a bit?" I glanced at the speed button, and followed with, "Oh, I see you already have". He was fair whizzing along now, and we had to break into a brisk stride to keep up with him... easier said than done for my uncle, who's on the list for a new hip!

After lunch, we decided to hunt out the Airborne Engineers memorial. Asking one of the guides, she pointed in the general direction where we'd find it, which was across the grass as the crow flew. Dad was now off-roading and loving every minute. I was trotting behind him, and my uncle had gone for a well-deserved sit down. When we reached the general area, our plan was thwarted as there was a ditch between us and our destination. If I hadn't changed direction, I'm pretty sure dad would have had a good go at crossing it though. Getting back on the path we followed it round. Heading round the corner, I was looking out for something that resembled a horse statue. Suddenly, I spotted it. It was huge. "This way dad" I pointed, "not far now", as we off-roaded across the grass once more in its general direction.

Reaching the statue, it was even more impressive up close. A huge Pegasus rearing up, with a Para to the front of it, hauling his parachute in. Standing before it, I said, "Here we are, dad, this is the Airborne one".

He gazed up in awe at the statue for a good few moments, then gave a strangled sob, and a tear rolled down his cheek. Furiously wiping it away, he sat and took in the splendour of the statue before us. He scooted up to the Pegasus, drinking it all in, and re-joined me at the bottom, just as my aunt caught up with us.

Looking at us both, then on to the memorial, he nodded, and said softly, "That's good".

It was now time to go home, so everyone got back on the coach after a thoroughly good day out and dad dozed contentedly all the way home.

Arriving back, we went up to his room, and I realised his TV was again frozen on a screen, happily not on any dodgy channels. I set about hunting for the remote control and found it in the bottom of the wardrobe. Turning the TV off at the plug and plugging in the aerial that he'd taken out reset it, and I found him a channel to sit and watch. Whilst playing hunt the remote, I found his new glasses which was an added bonus, so swapped these over with the antique ones he was wearing.

"Have you had a good day, dad?"

He looked peaceful, and I could tell he had.

Giving him a hug goodbye, I managed to knock his glasses off, and as they fell on the floor, the lens popped out.

Inner demon snorted with laughter and said, "I do not believe it!"

Happily, I managed to pop the lens back in, and I settled him down in his armchair to watch the programme.

"Do you fancy a beer, dad?" I asked.

I noted there was a sign above the fridge which now stated:

PLEASE MAKE SURE FRIDGE IS SET TO COLD

Getting a can out and pouring it into a glass I was happy to note that the beer was indeed cold.

I left him sitting comfortably in his armchair, correct glasses on, contentedly watching his TV having a cold beer.

A perfect end to a perfect day out.

*10 Airborne Engineers at the Arboretum*

A while after this, the Veteran's coffee morning group was organising another trip in a narrow boat along the canal. I'd had mine and dad's name on the list for ages and the big day finally arrived.

When I took him out on trips, I had now started to drive him to the destination and meet the others that had gone on the coach.

This served a couple of purposes. For one, I could factor in extra time to allow for getting him ready to leave the building, as invariably he'd still be eating his breakfast, or not ready to go, or would have forgotten that we were going anywhere at all. It also meant that the people on the coach trip wouldn't be waiting around for us to arrive.

Secondly, dad loved a trip out in the car since not being able to drive about himself. I've got a Beetle convertible, and without fail when dad sat in it, he'd tap the dashboard and mutter, "Nice motor". In warm weather I'd make a big event of putting the roof down for him. On colder days I'd make sure the heated seats were on as he always gave out a murmur of contentedness when the warmth kicked in. He'd give a little squirm in his seat followed by a "Hmmm". The smallest of things, but it made me smile.

I remember my brother telling me when he'd bought himself a new car. He picked dad up and took him for a spin in it. A fast spin down the lanes. He said that dad had been hanging on to the door handle for dear life and had absolutely loved it.

All the usual arrangements had been made. I'd called the home the day before, to ask them to make sure he was up and smart, and I'd arranged to pick him up at 8.30 am. The others were due to arrive at the marina at half 9, so realistically I had plenty of time if everything went to plan. Arriving at the home, I let myself in and travelled to his floor in the lift. A brief knock on his door, letting myself in, I was relieved to find him clean, smart, and ready to go.

"Come on, dad" I trilled. "We're off on a boat today. Are you ready to go?"

A confused expression furrowed his brow, and inner demon stood tentatively on the sidelines, knowing this could go either way.

"No" he said, shaking his head. In his hands were his electric shaver from the bathroom, his comb and his shoehorn.

He searched for the words, which finally came as "They come and take these. The people… take them."

Inner demon groaned and rolled her eyes skywards. I countered, "No, they don't dad. Nobody comes in to take things."

He looked adamant, waved the offending items at me, and repeated, "The people – they take these."

"Of all the blooming days!" Inner demon piped up. "Of all the blooming days!"

I glared across to silence her, and at that moment, I knew what I needed to do to get him out of the building on time.

"OK Dad" I ventured. "If the people come and look for your things, how about we hide them away until we get back? How would that work?"

His worried expression gently transformed into one of relief. Making a joke of it now, I opened his wardrobe, and continued, "Let's hide them in there for now – nobody would ever think of looking there! We can get them out again after the trip and put them away properly."

At this, he nodded his approval and handed them to me. I made a big show of hiding them under some clothes on the wardrobe shelf, shut the door firmly, and said, "Right, let's go on the trip!"

On the way downstairs to the car, I reflected on what had just happened, and realised that little by little, we were stepping into dad's world, and working with what made sense for him; instead of fighting against him. We were becoming more and more aware that his illness made him behave in certain ways. It wasn't dad being difficult or awkward, it was the Alzheimer's making him confused and paranoid. Little by little we were having to change our own behaviour to accommodate his, because there was absolutely no point at all in trying to reason with him. Plus, it was exhausting for everyone concerned and a complete waste of time and energy.

Maybe this comes naturally, with time.

We were soon on our way. The sun was shining, and it was a beautiful day for a canal boat trip. The lost minutes were soon made up, and we were back on track to meet up with the others at the marina.

We travelled along in amiable silence, listening to the radio.

Breaking the silence, I said, "You went on a boat trip last week, too, didn't you?"

Silence returned, and I could tell that he was thinking about this.

Finally, "Did I?"

"Yes," I continued. I called to see you on Friday, and they told me you'd gone off in the bus for a boat trip. You do get about, don't you!"

"I must have done, then." He replied thoughtfully.

Arriving at the marina at pretty much the same time as the coachload we got out of the car and I noticed that he hadn't got any socks on, just shoes.

There wasn't time to go back to fetch any, so I just hoped that nobody would notice, and he wouldn't get cold.

We were all soon seated on the boat and on our way chugging up the canal. Dad seemed very content, silently watching the bank go by. The others were striking up conversations, but he seems happy now with his own company and the thoughts in his head. Glancing over, I noticed that he had a little snooze from time to time too. After a peaceful couple of hours up and down the canal, it was soon time for us to disembark and travel to a pub in the next village for a spot of lunch. Settling dad back into my car, I arranged to follow behind the coach.

On the second leg of our journey, I remembered a story that he used to tell us about when he was a boy.

"Dad, do you remember telling us about when you took your duck for a walk on a bit of string?" I asked.

The all-familiar pause while he gathers his thoughts and words together.

"Yes", he said firmly. I knew he'd placed that memory.

"And you took it to the lake, and let it out for a swim?"

He's smiling and nodded, "yes."

"And a swan came swimming towards you, so you had to reel your duck in off the lake?"

He snorts, "Yes!"

"What was the duck's name, dad?"

There followed a silence, then dad blurted out the answer, as if it were the most obvious name in all the world, "Duck!"

I laughed, "So the duck was called Duck?"

"Yes" he replied. "I had ducks", he paused, "And rabbits".

All this slotted into place in my mind. "So, the duck wasn't a pet, you had a few of them?"

"Yes, and chickens"

"Did you eat them?"

"Yes" was the reply. "My dad was away."

Piecing together this scenario, I asked, "Was it your job to put the meat on the table?"

"Yes. My mam was at work".

"And it's right that after the war, your dad didn't come home until another three years later?"

"That's right."

Knowing that the war ended in 1945, and dad was born in 1935, it didn't take a genius to work out that at the tender age of 10 years old (and quite likely before), my dad was responsible for looking after the ducks, chickens and rabbits, and slaughter them accordingly so the family could eat meat.

This shouldn't have been such a stark realisation, thinking back. When we were children, my sister had two rabbits that got a bit over familiar with each other, and nature took its course. I vividly remember a pen full of rabbits in the garden, whose numbers were slowly dwindling. Asking dad at the time where the rabbits were going, he told us sagely that they were ill, and some had died. A while after that, after we'd tucked into chicken stew for the umpteenth time it seemed, dad clapped his hands together and announced, "Well, that's the last of the rabbits, then!" It would appear we had been unwittingly eating them. Maybe the 10-year-old inside dad looked at all the rabbits, and instantly thought, "food".

Pulling up behind the coach at the pub, lunch was enjoyable. I chatted to our fellow table guests, and dad ate his lunch in silence. Afterwards, we made the trip back home and dad had a well-deserved snooze.

Arriving back at his room, I retrieved his shaver, comb and shoehorn from the wardrobe and put them all back in their rightful places.

Going to turn the TV on, the remote control was nowhere to be found. I checked in all the usual places, and in doing so turned up a pair of his glasses in a case with a broken frame. "I'll take these and get them fixed for you, dad".

A staff member popped her head around the door to check we were alright, and I asked if she could have a hunt about for the missing TV remote. I also mentioned to her that he hadn't had any socks on that morning. She explained that he had refused to have any on, and when we inspected his feet further, it was more than apparent that his ankles were really swollen. If nothing else, we have learned that there's never such a thing as 'one job' where dad is involved. It always leads to something else.

I asked for him to be put onto the regular doctor's rounds, just to check if there was anything that could be done for his ankles, or if there was any underlying problem. Arriving home, I then ordered him some fully adjustable slippers, and some super stretchy socks, so he could be comfortable. I threw in some new pants for good measure to take down to him as soon as they arrive.

The slippers, socks and pants arrived a couple of days later with the sorcery that is online shopping, and I whizzed off to the home so he could get the benefit of them as soon as possible. Entering the big double doors, the receptionist greeted me with a warm smile. Handing her the items, I asked her if she could get the pants and socks labelled up for him, and I'd just be a minute to nip upstairs to see if the slippers fitted. Rather pleased with my purchases, I showed her the super stretchy socks, and how the slippers opened right out and were adjustable both sides of the foot and even the heel. It then occurred to me that due to the nature of her job, she's probably seen all these things a thousand times.

Reaching dad's door, I gave a little knock and let myself in. "Present time!" I announced. Dad took a moment to recognise who I was and smiled.

"First of all, I've had your glasses fixed!" I announced proudly, handing them to him. Popping them on his nose, he peered at me.

Kneeling down in front of his chair, I whipped the slippers out of their box. "Look" I said, "New slippers for you too!"

Pointing to the shoes he was wearing, he replied, "But I've got…"

"Yes, I know you've got your shoes, but these are comfy slippers for when you are indoors." I continued, "We just need to check that they fit, and I can get your name put in them, so everyone knows that they are yours."

Removing his shoe, I noted that his feet were still swollen, and the slippers would be a godsend if they fit him. Undoing the Velcro, I showed him how the slippers opened right out, so he only had to pop his foot into them. This he duly did, and I showed him how they could now be tweaked at the back and over the sides.

"What do you think?"

His face showed instant contentment, and I knew they were a good fit and he liked them. "Good" he murmured.

"Brilliant news! I'll just nip back down and get them labelled up for you, and you can have them on later."

With that, I scooped up the slippers and headed off back to reception. Handing over the slippers, I remarked, "They are perfect. I think they will be really comfy for him."

Back in his room, I plonked myself down on his bed.

"So how have you been? Been up to much?"

He looked vaguely puzzled as though he was dredging his brain for the information.

"Don't think so," he said slowly.

"You went out the other day with Aunt Christine, didn't you? Looked like you had a lovely time."

His brow furrowed, and I knew he was thinking something like, "I did?"

Whipping out my phone, I showed him some pictures my aunt had sent through. "Yes, here you are. They took you to the regimental museum."

He gazed at the photos of him sitting with my aunt and uncle in the coffee shop, and the penny dropped. "Yes," he nodded, "I did."

Dad and Aunt Christine have always been very close, and you can see that they clearly adore one another. When dad was posted in Germany, he heard that my aunt, also in the Army, was unhappy with her current posting. He arranged for her to be posted out to Germany with him, where she met our would-be Uncle Les. The story goes that dad, as a newly promoted Sergeant Major approached Les, saying "I believe you are going out with my sister. Well, you'd better look after her, or else!" Les obviously heeded that advice as my aunt and uncle are still going strong to this very day.

Dad then continued with the story he tells us every time we visit, "That road out there," and paused like he couldn't quite find the words, "That road… I'll show you."

Heaving himself out of the chair, he shuffled out of the door and along to the end of the corridor where there's a U-shape bench and windows to each side. Turning to the front, he pointed to the school playground.

"Yes," I said. "That's where you used to go to school, isn't it? You used to cross that road and come down that alley way, and there was your school." He smiled and nodded.

Turning to the left, he pointed to the road. "And that road…"

"Is where you used to live, I know dad. Lots of memories along here for you, aren't there?"

"And at the top…" He did a hand movement that went straight up and turned right. I knew he was referring to where his house is.

"Yes," I said gently. "Your house is there." I continued, "But you don't live there anymore, do you? You live here now."

He nodded slowly, took a last look out of the window and ambled back towards his room. He rarely asks to go home now; I think he knows that it's no longer possible. And he seems happy here. He's clean, well fed and all the staff love him. The Facebook page for the home is testament to that!

Sitting back on his bed, I set up the digital photo frame that he'd unplugged and put in the wardrobe and speeded up the picture display for him. We watched the pictures tick round for a while, and every now and then he'd spot himself and point at the photo. Reaching for one of the photos in frames along the desk, I picked up the one with myself and my brothers and sisters on.

"Who are these, Dad?"

Gently touching the people in the picture one by one, he replied, "They are mine,".

"Yes, but do you know their names?"

A puzzled expression followed, and he pointed to the picture of me.

"Yes, that's me… what's my name?"

He laughed because he and I both knew that he didn't know the answer.

"I'm Lynnette."

"Ahh Lynnette, that's right."

I continued naming my brothers and sisters from the photo, and he nodded slowly with a half-smile on his face.

At that moment, there was a knock on the door and a friendly face popped her head round.

"Are you coming for lunch, George?" she asked

Dad's eyes lit up, and he gave a quick nod in reply.

"Come on then dad," I said. I'll walk you down.

Entering the dining room, I asked where he wanted to sit, and he pointed to where a gentleman was sitting in the far corner.

"Is that your mate, dad?"

The gents gave each other a wave. I hugged dad tightly goodbye and he ambled across the room to have his lunch.

This was a good visit. Well, apart from the remote control is still missing, but you can't have everything.

As it's highly impractical to be turning dad's room upside down every time we visit in the now all too common 'hunt the remote' game, I decided to just get a universal one, so if the old one turned up, at least there would be a spare. Looking online, it appeared the mission might not be as straightforward as first thought (surprise, surprise!). Many of the universal ones tuned themselves in from the existing remote control, which could be problematic if it were indeed, properly lost and not just in his pant drawer or something. One time, his teeth ended up in the laundry room, so really, anything is possible!

Refining my search, I came across a universal remote control that not only tuned in straight from the TV set, but only had a couple of big, bold buttons on it. One for on/off, one for volume control and one to change the channel. Nothing could be more perfect. Even dad would be able to get his head around that, surely! Rather pleased with myself, and 30 quid lighter I popped it into my virtual basket.

*Spoiler alert – it's still not my money, I paid with his card.

A couple of days later, it duly arrived, which was impeccable timing as it happened, as my sister and I had a review meeting at the care home the very next day.

In preparation for the visit, I called for my sister a little earlier so we could double check any points we wanted to mention. In almost one swift move, she popped the kettle on and whipped out a notepad and pen… she does love a little list! Over our brew, she began to put pen to paper.

"Feet", she announced, and the list was born.

"Agree", I said. We both knew we've mentioned dad's swollen feet on a couple of occasions and asked him to be seen by the visiting doctor. "Do you think the doctor has been yet?" I asked out loud.

"We'll soon find out," came the reply.

"Outings," I added. "Yes," she nodded. If there's a trip out, we want him on it."

The list slowly took shape, and the time came for us to visit the home.

On arrival, we were ushered upstairs, where a senior member of staff would conduct dad's review. Out came his file, and we sat around a small table.

"So," said the senior. "How do you think your dad has settled in?"

We had a short conversation about how pleased we were with his general health and wellbeing. We noted how he was obviously eating well and looked well looked after. We added that the staff at the home were lovely, and really interacted with the residents.

Seeming pleased with these points, she added, "So, is there anything else you'd like to talk about?"

Needing no further encouragement, my sister whipped out the list and placed it on the table. "There are just a few things we'd like to mention," she said.

Starting at the top, she asked, "Has the doctor been to see his feet? They have been swollen for a while, and we don't like to think that he is uncomfortable."

"Hmmm, not sure," came the reply. "I don't think he's complained his feet are sore."

I answered, "Dad is ex-Army and ex Airborne Engineers. His leg could be hanging off and he wouldn't complain about it. He would never make a fuss. He'd just get on with it."

"Ahh, I see," she replied. I've just come off a run of nights, so I'm not all that familiar with what everyone is up to on this floor at the moment. Let me check his notes and see what's what."

With that, she opened dad's care plan folder and flipped through a few sheets. Running her finger down the page, she stopped halfway down.

"Hmmm… yes, here it is," she said. "I can see that you asked for the Dr to visit, and it says here your dad had some blood tests this morning." Glancing across at the sheet she was reading from and impressed with the level of detail in his care notes, I countered, "That's good news then. I added, "With the blood tests, would they show up anything else? We're aware that dad's memory is slowly getting worse, and he's been on the same low dose of medication for ages now. He may need different medication by now."

"Fair point," came the reply, as she made a note on the review sheet. "I'll ask them to do some fuller blood tests, to look for memory issues too."

We then mentioned about the trips. We explained that although dad seems happy and settled in the home, he's always been fiercely independent, so any chance of getting him out and about would be really appreciated, by us, and more importantly, by him. Even just a wander in the park would be great for him. She added the requests to his notes.

Next down the list… trumpet.

"Does dad play his trumpet?" My sister asked. "Just that a couple of times we have asked him, and he seems to think he isn't allowed." She continued, "We have asked at the desk, and everyone says that they love hearing him play."

I joined the conversation, "We have a couple of thoughts of why he might think that he's not allowed. In his old house, the neighbours used to bang on the wall when he played, so he might be remembering that." I continued, "Or… it could even be something daft like he has a memory of his mum telling him to be quiet as a child. Either way, if you could encourage him to play, he'd really enjoy that."

Adding trumpet playing to the list, she asked, "Anything else?"

"Beer." We replied. "Beer?" she asked.

We explained that dad loved a decent pint, and asked, if they could encourage him to have a glass in the evening. We knew that there was a sign up to make sure it wasn't set to hot, but for someone to pour him a glass in the evening would be lovely for him.

She added 'beer in the evening' to her notes too and asked if we had anything more to add.

"Just one last thing," I reached into my bag and produced the new remote control.

"He's forever losing his remote, and we don't like to think that he can't watch TV and might be sitting on his own in his room, so we got him a new one."

She looked quizzically at the box on the desk.

"It looks quite good," I continued. "Apparently it can tune to any TV, and even if his remote turns up, they'll both still work."

My sister chimed in, "Could you ask the maintenance chap to sort it for him please?"

"And can you label it too please?" I asked. "It might stop him hiding it!"

The meeting ended and my sister and I headed off down the corridor to say a quick hello to dad. It was nearly lunch time, and all the residents were slowly making their way down to the dining room. Reaching dad's room, we found him straightening things out in there before he left. We think he does this, so he has some chance of remembering where things are. But this sometimes works against him. One day you can go, and all his photos are out on the side. The next day they are all neatly stacked up in a drawer. He seems to spend lots of time arranging and rearranging his stuff, so it's no wonder that he's forever losing things.

He also has a habit of putting things neatly on the top shelf in his wardrobe and meticulously lining them all up. We think this might be a memory of his Army days where everything would have to be ship shape before an inspection.

"Hi dad," We chimed, "how are you?"

He furrowed his brow, and that familiar brief expression of confusion was followed by one of recognition, and he'd placed who we were. Relieved, we each hugged him and asked how he was, told him he was looking well, asked what he'd been up to, and all the usual topics of conversation.

"It's lunch time now, dad." I said.

"We'll walk you down to the dining room," added my sister.

We all began the slow walk down the corridor, when suddenly, dad turned on his heel and headed back to his room. Waiting for him, he emerged a few moments later with his jacket over his arm.

"What are you doing?" we asked? "It's lunch time now."

Shaking his head, he replied, "No. I'm coming with you."

My sister and I caught each other's eye, with a mixture of guilt and sadness. Dad couldn't come with us, as we both had to go back to work. But there he stood in front of us, all ready for a walk out.

"It's lunch time now," we said softly. "We'll come and take you out later."

Reaching the dining room, we gestured to a member of staff what had happened. "Don't worry, leave it with me," her face replied.

Greeting dad warmly, she placed his jacket gently over the arm of a chair.

"Come on, George" as she took his arm and guided him to his table. "It's your favourite for lunch today."

My sister and I sat down for a while so he could still see us, and when he began to eat his lunch, we made our way over to say goodbye. Hugging him, we assured him we'd be back to see him soon, and he smiled and nodded. Looking back as we approached the lift, we saw that he was tucking into his lunch, and it was obvious that he'd forgotten all about the jacket, and all about the trip out.

Getting into the car, we looked at each other with a dirty great cloud of guilt hanging over us.

"God, this is awful," she said.

"I know." I replied.

Then followed the discussion that we've had many, many times. What else could we have done? Dad wasn't safe at home, so him living there was ruled out. I'd thought about him moving into my house, but that wasn't an option either. Mine is an old house full of steps and levels; we've had perfectly mobile people fall headfirst into the bathroom. Plus the fact he'd no doubt be letting himself out and wandering off, and chances were, he wouldn't remember the way back or would turn up at his old house.

My sister had even toyed with the idea of extending her house to accommodate a 'grandad flat', but we agreed that would be just moving all the problems we were facing with dad's health from one house to another. We had to come to terms with the fact that dad has an illness. An illness with no cure. An illness that was only ever going to get gradually worse and never, ever better.

Although we knew the answers to the conversation, we still went through the motions of having it; almost like we were checking off a list of possible and convincing ourselves that we'd done the right thing.

With heavy hearts, we both went back to work.

*11 Me, dad and my younger sister Sharon*

A couple of days later, my phone pinged. It was a text from our aunt. She'd been to see dad that afternoon and was concerned as he seemed very down in the dumps and had a rattling, phlegmy cough. I asked if she had spoken to the staff, and she replied that yes, she had. Apparently, there was some bug going around. I texted my sister and brother, just to let them know what was happening.

My sister said that she'd call the home in the morning, to see what the situation was, and my aunt told us she was popping back in the morning too and would keep us informed of how he was.

As we were now concerned about dad's cough, my sister called the home to see how he was getting on. They told her that he was still chesty, but he hadn't complained at all.

That's just the thing she explained wearily once again. Dad's a veteran. Ex Army, Ex Airborne Engineers, A soldier through and through. Blah blah blah. He never complains about anything.

After arranging a doctor call out to check him over it transpired that he had a chest infection, and a course of antibiotics was prescribed. The day after, my aunt visited again and reported back cheerfully that he was already much better in himself, and a bit chirpier, which was great news all round.

The next day I had an hour free, so decided to pop down to see him, and pay a visit. The sun was shining, and it was a beautiful day, so I took the opportunity to load the car up with our little dog Ruby, planning to get him out for a breath of fresh air, and a wander round the park.

Arriving at the home, Ruby was star of the show. She's a chihuahua crossed with a Jack Russell and, although I'm biased, she's the cutest little dog ever. With a friendly temperament and a furiously waggy tail, the old folks loved her. It took me a while to get down the corridor to dad's room, as she was being called over here there and everywhere for strokes and fuss. Which she wasn't complaining about one bit.

Reaching dad's room, I gave a little knock and let myself in. There he was, sitting in the chair, looking out of the window. The weather by now had suddenly turned a tad gloomier, a sign the autumn nights are definitely drawing in. Ruby launched herself into the room and busied herself with all the brand-new sniffs and smells.

"Hi Dad," I said. He narrowed his eyes, and I gave him a moment to place who I was. His expression shortly turned to one of recognition, and he replied with a nod, "Alright."

"You've had a cough, haven't you?"

"Yes," he replies.

"And the doctor came to see you," I continued.

Another slight nod, "Yes."

"And are you starting to feel better now?"

A slight smile twitched at the corners of his mouth. "Yes."

Noting that his TV wasn't on, I asked, "Did you get the new remote control?" Again, a look of puzzlement. "For the telly, dad. I got you a new control so you could work the telly better. It's white." At that I mimed holding a remote control pointed to the TV, and my thumb went into some serious up and down button pressing actions.

Cocking his head to one side and thinking slightly, he heaved himself out of his chair and shuffled over to the wardrobe. On the shelf I spotted his pyjamas, and a various assortment of objects beneath. He reached in and patted his hands around in there. Pulling out his shaver that he'd unplugged from the bathroom, he showed it to me.

"No dad, that's your shaver. You're looking for your remote. It's the thing that turns the telly on. It's white." I continued, "Your shaver needs to be on charge else it won't work. Let me put it back in the bathroom for you." I gently took it from his hands and popped it back on its charger.

He then shuffled a few more objects around on the shelf.

"Do you want me to have a look?" I asked.

At that, he popped his head around the side of the wardrobe door and handed me the remote control.

*Note to self. If anything goes missing, look on that shelf of delights first.

"Brilliant dad. Well done. Look, it's a new one with just a couple of buttons so you can work it." I turned it over and pointed to the reverse. "Look, it's even got your name on it, so everyone knows it's yours and not to move it out of your room." I placed it on the coffee table next to the chair.

"Do you fancy a wander round the park?"

His face said 'definitely'.

"You'll need your coat on then, it's gone a bit cold outside all of a sudden."

Fetching his coat off the hook on the door, I helped him into it and helped zip him up. With that, we were off back down the corridor, via everybody wanting to fuss the dog on the way. They obviously loved having a waggy, licky little dog around the place, and I made a mental note to take her back in another day.

Shuffling out of the main entrance, I took my time to let dad walk at his own pace. Down the alleyway, and into the park we proceeded along the path. About 50 meters in, we spotted a bench. "Do you want to carry on walking, or sit?" I asked.

His hand waved towards the bench, which I took to mean 'sit' so I cleared some leaves off and we sat down. Sitting in comfortable silence, we watched the world, and a few dog walkers go by. He did his normal conversation of pointing to different areas of the park. I played along by having the conversation he was trying to have, only the out loud version. I have had this conversation many many times and I'm word perfect now.

"Yes, the swings used to be there…. And that was where the cricket pavilion was. Yes, they play cricket on here, don't they? Bet you can see them from up in your room." And so we went on.

A little while later, I said, "Fancy a wander back, now? It's getting colder."

"Yes," he replied, and we slowly made our way out of the park. Halfway up the alley, I looked at him, and asked, "Dad, how old are you?"

His brow furrowed, and the answer came, "I don't know. How old am I?"

"You're 84!" I exclaimed. "Who would believe it?"

"84…" he repeated slowly to himself as though he couldn't quite believe that either.

"Yes, 84! And how old do you think I am?"

Scrunching up his face, he peered at me intently. He had no idea. "Have a guess dad. How old would you think?"

Furrowing his brow, "30." Came the definite answer.

Laughing, I said, "Actually, I'm 50 dad, but I'll take that! Fancy being 30 again!"

Arriving back at his room, I helped him back out of his coat and hung it up. His expression hardened as if he'd remembered something.

The words came slowly "The people." He waved at the assortment of coats. "The people…"

We've also had this conversation a fair few times now, so I kind of know what he's saying.

"They take things?" I offered.

"Yes!"

Gently, I held his arm, and replied, "People don't take things here dad. All your stuff is safe here. You are safe here."

Then thinking that he might have actually lost something, I had a quick frisk of all his coat pockets. Lo and behold, his glasses were in one of the pockets, so I whipped them out and handed them to him. "Wonder what they are doing in there, dad." I joked. "Here you are, keep them safe. Maybe put them in that cupboard?"

He did just that and I followed up, "Before I go, shall we get your telly working?"

Sitting on the end of the bed, I pressed the on button. Sure enough, the TV sprang into life. "Look dad," I showed him the remote. "This only has a couple of buttons. One for on and off, up and down the channels, and louder and softer. Easy for you."

Scrolling through the channels to satisfy myself that it worked, I landed on a programme that looked half interesting. "Want to watch this one?"

He nodded.

"Right, I need to shoot off now. You have a nice evening, and I'll see you very soon."

Hugging him goodbye, he squeezed a little tighter than normal. He pulled away and held my shoulders and looked deep into my eyes.

"And you…" he said softly. "Have a nice life."

I smiled and replied, "I'll really try to do that, dad."

And with that, I kissed his cheek, gathered the dog back, and left him to his programme.

*12 Dad and my younger brother Charles, in the band*

The following Sunday was Remembrance Parade. Being of military background, this is an occasion that is important to our family, and we try to attend every year. My brother, who's in the Army had arranged to travel up the night before with his family and stay over at ours, to leave plenty of time to collect dad for the parade in the town centre. Not to miss an opportunity for a get together, we'd invited my sister and her family up too, for a bite to eat and a few drinks.

On the morning of the parade, our house was a hive of activity, with everyone busy with their own tasks for the morning. My brother was polishing his belt and shoes on the kitchen island, my husband was rustling up a full English and pancakes, I was chief tea masher, and the children were in the front room, glued to some syrupy, cheesier than a chunk of cheese YouTube channel, where you watch someone play a video game. Who knew there was such a thing?!

Before long, in between cups of tea, ironing uniform, feeding the family and getting dressed, we were all suited and booted and ready to leave. Picking up his keys, my brother entered the lounge and announced, "Right, I'm off to fetch dad. Meet you at the War Memorial."

His daughter, who I might add is absolutely as cute as a button clapped eyes on him, looked him slowly up and down and chimed, "I didn't know you were in the Army!" I do hope she meant to say that she didn't know that he would be wearing his uniform today, otherwise his whole career has been one big fat lie.

The plan was that we were going to lurk near the parade route in case Charles couldn't park the car so he could drop dad off with us and we could walk him the short way into the park to the War Memorial. Leaving the house, we all took a slow wander into town. Rounding the corner and approaching the park entrance, we spotted Charles' car. We helped dad out of the car and my brother went off to park it. We couldn't have timed it better. Relieved to see that he looked lovely and smart in his best overcoat, complete with poppy and was even wearing his Airborne Engineers red beret, we began the slow walk into the park.

With dad being quite unsteady on his feet now, combined with a walk up a slippery ramp made for a hairy few minutes. With good use of his walking stick and all of us supporting his other side, we finally made it into the memorial area and located a bench for him to be able to sit down. A lady came round, handing out the order of service sheets, and she cheerfully handed each of us one. Dad promptly folded his up and slid it in his pocket, never to see light of day again.

The service began and dad stood to attention while all the military organisations marched in; from the Air Cadets to the Sea Cadets, to the Marines to the Cubs and Scouts, I was proud of my town for putting such an effort into our mark of respect.

My aunt stood next to dad and opened her order of service, and dad looked round with a definite look that said, "Why don't I have one?". She offered hers up for him to share and he silently followed along with the proceedings. After the Last Post and the Two Minutes Silence came the laying of the wreaths, followed by a hymn. My aunt pointed to the words to keep their place in the service, and I could hear dad singing along softly beside me.

During the hymn I noticed that he got slightly more confident as each verse progressed, as the words were given to him on the sheet, and he didn't have to fight through the fog in his brain to produce them. I got the distinct impression that he'd really quite enjoyed a jolly old sing song.

At the end of the service, we all began to file out of the War Memorial to make our way into town to see the parade march past. With dad holding onto the handrail, walking stick firmly in his other hand, we slowly but surely made our descent into the park. Watching dad gingerly yet determinedly make his way down the steep path, I realised with a pang that this may well be the last time we'd be able to physically bring him to the Remembrance Service.

Reaching the bottom, me, my brother and dad made the short but slow journey across the car park and into the High Street, where we could hear the band approaching. Arriving just in time, we secured dad a space at the front of the crowd so he could have a good view. As the parade marched past, dad drank it all in, standing tall and proud, nodding his acknowledgement and silent thanks to the various troops and groups. Once passed, the crowd began to disperse, and the High Street slowly emptied. Re-joining the rest of our family who we'd lost during the walk in, we all remarked what a great turnout it had been, and what a nice service.

"I'll get the car," my brother announced, "And meet you at the top. OK?"

With that, he spun on his heel and strode back off across the park.

"Right then dad," I said, "Time to get you back for lunch now."

He looked a tad confused. "Stanley Road," he said.

"You used to live there, yes." I replied.

He looked at his feet, and countered, "How are we getting there?"

It clicked into place. He thought he was going back to his childhood home for lunch and was worried about how he was going to be able to walk there.

"Don't worry," I reassured him. "Charles will fetch the car and he will take you. But you don't live in Stanley Road anymore. You live at the bottom. Do you remember? Where the pub used to be?"

Dad furrowed his brow. I repeated. "It's OK. All we need to do is walk up to there," I pointed to the top of the road about 50 meters away, "and Charles will bring his car there. He is going to take you back for your lunch."

We began the slow walk to the top of the road, and as Charles neared us, I pointed, and said, "Here he is now."

Opening the car door, dad took a couple of attempts to get in the passenger seat, and we could tell this was an effort for him. Finally in, we buckled him up, said our goodbyes and they were off.

A couple of weeks after, as it was getting near to Christmas, my elder brother messaged to say he was coming down to drop off some presents. He suggested that he would go to visit dad first, then head up to our house a little later.

"Why don't you fetch dad and bring him here?" I suggested. "He'll like a ride out, and I can put some food on."

"Perfect." Replied my brother. "See you then!"

I told my younger sister and brother that he was visiting, and before we knew it, we had an impromptu engagement for a houseful of people. A Christmas present drop had swiftly morphed into a gathering!

Everyone arrived at the given time and drinks were flowing for the non-drivers amongst us. Sitting dad down next to the table we made sure he had a plate of food and a pint. Quite content sitting there, I'd catch him looking around the room, settling his eyes on someone, and there was almost like an 'aha' moment when he realised that he knew all these people. The family made general conversation with him, and his answers were mainly nods or indecipherable mumbles. But he seemed more than comfortable to be here.

Before long, nature called, and he hoisted himself off the chair and slowly headed towards the back door where he'd remembered the outside toilet was.

I caught both my brothers' eyes and motioned that he would need some help. Getting to the outside loo involved navigating some pretty steep steps in the dark, and there would be nothing worse than dad having a tumble down them. At that point, I realised once and for all that for any good intentions I may have had in the past of having him live with us, it simply would have been impossible. He wouldn't last five minutes.

Returning from his visit, he sat back down as before. My sister sat beside him, and I could hear that they were going over the same conversations of where he was born, where he used to live, and how he didn't live there anymore. She then went on to say that we were looking for a family to live in that house so we could put some pennies into his bank. Remarkably, he seemed very accepting of this. Whether he will remember tomorrow I have no idea, but for now it was all OK with him.

All around the family were chatting and catching up, and the mood was light.

It struck us that he used to be the life and soul of any party or family gathering. He used to have an irrepressible zest for life and was always laughing and joking. At gatherings you'd hear him having a heated debate with someone, often about social issues or politics. A staunch Tory all his life, but nowadays had no clue about who was running the country. Quick witted and full of fun, with always a quick word and a dance to be had, now struggled to get simple words and phrases out.

I cannot emphasise enough what a cruel, cruel disease this is, and when I look at the shadow of the man he used to be standing before me. it makes me want to weep.

After a little while I noticed he looked a bit agitated, tapping the chair beside him, and looking around a little furtively. Sitting beside him, I asked, "Are you OK dad?"

Furrowing his brow, he slowly replied, "No… not really?"

"What do you need? More food? Another beer? Can we get you anything?"

Carefully considering his answer, he said "Where. Is. My. Bed?"

"Are you ready to go back now, dad?" I continued, "Have you had enough?"

"Yes. I am" came the reply.

My elder brother was making moves to leave at this point, and I asked him if he'd mind taking dad back on his way.

For the first time that I can remember, dad had been quite ready to leave and go back; another sign he is more settled now. He'd enjoyed his time with us, but he didn't want to stay. He wanted to go back to what was familiar to him. His own room, with his bed and TV and all his personal pictures and photos.

And I felt a wave of relief. After this long and difficult journey, we seem to have come around a corner. Yes, dad still has Alzheimer's, and still can't live alone in his house, but it almost felt that another layer of the weight had been lifted. He was OK there. That was his home now. Yes, he will still do daft things like lose stuff or unplug his TV aerial, but he's happy to be there. And if he is content, we are content too.

Getting him ready to go back to the home, we all kissed and hugged him goodbye, and my brother and sister-in-law drove him away.

*13 Dad and Charles at Remembrance Parade*

A couple of weeks later, collecting him for Veteran's coffee morning, I spotted he was wearing his super expandable slippers, which I haven't seen him in before. Arriving just as he was finishing off his breakfast, I also noticed he was wearing just a jumper with no shirt underneath. Pleased that I had plenty of time to get him sorted and away, we made the slow walk up the corridor to his room, to find his shoes and shirt.

Sitting him in the chair, I gently took off his slippers, and noted once more his swollen foot that looked bigger than ever. This was confirmed when after no amount of shoehorning, wiggling and prising, was his left shoe ever going to go on today.

"You'll have to wear your slippers today, dad," I said gently.

He looked at his feet and was obviously puzzled as to why on earth we would be going outside anywhere just in slippers.

"It's OK though" I reassured him. Nobody will notice, as they are dark and almost look like shoes. Best to have you comfy."

Moving on to his shirt, I helped him out his jumper with the Royal Engineers logo emblazoned on it and guided him into a clean shirt. Remembering my brother had bought him a lovely new jumper for Christmas, embroidered with the Airborne Engineers logo, I asked him if he fancied wearing it today. The jumper was a great choice for a present, as it's a standard joke that whenever pictures appear of him on the home's Facebook page, he's always wearing the same old jumper; a bit like a game of 'Where's Wally', really.

Fishing the new jumper out of the wardrobe, I waved it in front of him. "This one that George bought you – do you want to wear this today?" Pointing at logo on the front of it, I continued, "Look, it's got the Para badge on too."

Recognising the logo, he slowly smiled and nodded, and I proceeded to help him into the new jumper. It soon became evident that this was not going to be at all easy, and all too late it became obvious that said new jumper was a tad too small. We only realised this, however, after I'd wrestled him into it, and his head popped out of the neck hole. The neck was tight, and dad looked like a distressed tortoise.

Trying not to laugh, I said, "It's a bit too tight, isn't it?"

Wide eyed, dad gave out a strangled little nod.

Now, if getting the thing on was a struggle, getting it off was an entirely different kettle of fish. I pulled on the sleeves to try to release his arms, but the thing was stuck tight. Eventually, with much pulling, prodding, and brute force, the jumper popped back off, and I quickly returned it to the wardrobe.

Laughing, I turned back to him, "Well, that was a struggle, wasn't it!"

I quickly located a replacement jumper and helped him into it.

His hands fluttered up to his hair, which, with all the jumper friction was sticking up in all directions, like a mad professor.

Checking the bathroom, I hunted around for his comb, which was nowhere to be seen. Of course, his shaver and comb were always hidden in the wardrobe in case anyone fancied coming in to steal them! Looking there, I quickly located it, handed it to him and watched as he shuffled into the bathroom to comb his hair back down to respectable.

Returning from the bathroom, I remarked, "That's better dad. You look lovely and smart."

He smiled slightly to himself and puffed out his chest.

On the way out, I noted to the receptionist I'd seen his foot was still swollen and asked if she could add him to the list for the doctor when he next called. She noted this down on the pad, and glad he was going to be seen, I really hoped they could get to the bottom of it.

We continued off to the Veteran's Coffee Morning, where I sat dad down at the table, got him a drink and continued to serve refreshments to all the others. When I first took him to the coffee mornings, he had a decent level of conversation in him. Now, it's like someone has sucked all his words clean out of his body. He sits, drinks coffee and just takes in the atmosphere. The regulars there are very kind, and always make sure to include him, knowing full well they will just get the odd nod or shake of his head in reply. And as I predicted, nobody noticed he only had his slippers on, which was a blessing.

Little did we know then this would be dad's last outing.

A couple of days after, my sister called with an update on his health.

He had a follow up memory assessment, which he had failed dismally. The disease seems to be really taking hold now, and he's gone from middle stage Alzheimer's to late stage, so it would appear that the journey is now well on its way with no turning back. He had a deprivation of liberty report and the findings were heart-breaking. Dad is officially unable to live anywhere other than a nursing home. He is incapable of making any kind of decisions for himself and needs around the clock care.

We've all noticed the subtle changes, but it's very sobering to have the experts confirm it. We have a meeting with the doctor soon, to talk about dad's ongoing care plan, and what happens next.

Apparently, dad has something called edema, which is swelling of the feet and ankles. The home has changed his bed to one that can elevate his feet, to help reduce the swelling as he sleeps.

And then one day, everything changed. Not just for us, for the whole world. Coronavirus 19; some mystery deadly virus that originated in China was sweeping wildly across the world and was out of control.

Dad's care home made the agonising decision to stop all visits. Residents would be kept inside and kept safe but were out of bounds to the outside world. We really did think that it would be for a couple of weeks – a month at maximum and then life would revert to normal. I'd made a photo story book for dad's upcoming birthday, written like a children's book telling the story of his life, with pictures of his family, his wives, children, grandchildren and great grandchildren. He always loved welcoming the little ones into the family and loved the days when my nephews took their families to visit him with his ever-expanding number of great grandchildren.

When new babies arrived into the family he'd hold them in his arms and press a silver coin into the palm of their tiny hands, wrapping their little fingers around it to hold it tight. Without fail he'd announce "He/she is a little Bobby Dazzler!". I remember him rocking my baby brother to sleep, singing 'You are my sunshine'. All three verses and he'd be sound asleep.

When the visiting lockdown was announced I immediately took the book down to the home, in the hope that while we weren't allowed to visit, he would be able to look in the book and remember who we were, and maybe even more importantly, who *he* was. Then when we were allowed back in, we could pick up where we all left off and normal service would be resumed. But that time never came. The lockdown was extended and extended; the weeks turned into months, and as it turned out we couldn't celebrate his 85th birthday with him. Never mind we thought, we'll have a great big celebration once this is all over and we'll all make it up to him. On his birthday, his photo was on the Facebook page and the care home had obviously made a lot of effort to celebrate it with him. There he was, blowing out candles on an enormous cake, surrounded by residents we recognised.

I called my sister to make sure she'd seen the picture. Studying it, we remarked that 'something wasn't quite right'. Was his hair was combed the wrong way? Was it the angle of the photo? Then we spotted it. His watch was practically hanging off his wrist. He was losing weight.

We know that losing weight can be part of the illness – goodness knows, the illness has been a part of many an internet search. But was his weight loss due to the illness or him pining away with nobody to visit him? Had he given up? We called the home and noted our concerns and they assured us they would do everything in their power to encourage him to eat.

From that point his weight loss sped up and literally spiralled out of control. My sister had daily conversations and updates with the care home. The weight was literally dropping off him and it seemed there was nothing they could do. His illness had accelerated faster than anyone could ever have predicted. He wasn't eating. He was shutting down. We also had to face the stark reality that even if he did start eating and gained weight, he would never get better. He would never again be a well man. He would always have Alzheimer's. This cruel disease had finally clamped her claws well and truly into our dad, and this was the start of the point of no return.

One day my sister and I were in the park under his window and were convinced that we caught sight of him at the window. Ringing the home, we asked if he could be brought to the window just so that we could wave and reassure him that we were still there and hadn't abandoned him. The side door of the home opened and one of the staff made his way gravely towards us.

"I'm so sorry," he said. "That wasn't your dad at the window. He is in bed and too frail to be moved."

With each day came the news that his condition was worsening, and we had to face the agonising reality we were going to lose him, and the time wasn't going to be too far away. In truth I think we also realised that we had been slowly losing him for the past few years. Little by little, our dad had been slipping away from us.

Knowing that we weren't allowed to see him was heart-breaking, but we knew that a member of staff in the home was with him 24 hours a day, even sleeping on a mattress on his bedroom floor. Knowing he was never alone and always had someone by his side was a huge comfort.

A couple of days later my phone rang and it was my sister. I will never forget the sound of her heaving sobs. In between these she managed to tell me that she had been trying to call me, but she couldn't get through. That the home had told her that someone should go in to say our final goodbyes. That she'd had to make the decision to go in case we missed our chance. She was in the car park of the home.

Dropping everything and dashing there in my car, I met her outside. Inconsolable was an understatement. She had been allowed fifteen minutes with him. In full protective clothing she had told him that we all loved him so very much, but if it was his time, then it was alright for him to go. She said he squeezed her hand which was a sign that he knew she was there and that he understood. We couldn't even hug to comfort one another as the country was still in lock down and socially distancing. Standing apart in the car park for goodness knows how long, we shed silent tears with the knowledge that our dad wouldn't be with us for very much longer.

Only one visitor was allowed in and that slot had been taken. The rest of us never saw him again.

Arriving back home, I emotionally called the home and asked them to put the phone to his ear as I urgently needed to talk to him. They duly did and I told him again how much we all loved him. I then went on to tell him that Sharon and I had spoken to our mums – mine was his first wife, Sharon's was his second. I told him that we'd asked them to both look after him and be waiting for him to arrive. I told him how much we would miss him and what a brilliant father he had been to all of us. After I'd finished babbling on, I heard a barely audible "Yes."

I hung up the phone and the tears came.

The next evening, going to bed as normal, I woke up suddenly at about half past eleven. Shooting out of bed, I just knew I had to talk to dad.

Apologising to the lady on reception about how late it was but I stressed that I really needed to speak to him. They took the phone to his room and put the receiver to his ear. His breathing was laboured. Heavy and slow.

Once again, I told him how very, very loved he was by all of the family. Then for reasons I still can't explain to this day, and willing my voice not to shake, I began to sing to him.

*You are my sunshine, my only sunshine*

*You make me happy when skies are grey*

*You'll never know dear, how much I love you*

*Please don't take my sunshine away*


*The other night dear, as I lay dreaming*

*I dreamt that you had gone away*

*You'll never know dear, how much I love you*

*Please don't take my sunshine away*


The song that he used to sing to us as children. The song that soothed us off to sleep.

The next morning, we learned that he had passed away peacefully during the night. Just two and a half years from his diagnosis with Alzheimer's disease, and less than a year after we had to move him into a home, our handsome, forthright, intelligent father with his irrepressible zest for life had slipped away for the very last and final time.

His journey had ended. Our world went quiet.

*14 Dad on my wedding day*

## You can fall through cracks in the system

Dad was first diagnosed by his GP who referred him on to the memory clinic. We'd duly attend all our appointments where he'd have to try to draw clocks and answer questions. Each time we went he failed dismally. When the memory clinic could do no more, they referred him back to his GP. The GP system don't call you back in for checks. It almost felt like we were floating around in a system that was completely alien to us, and that didn't know what to do with us.

We had no idea if any support was available or how we might access this. All the life decisions we had to make, we had to make as a family. We basically had no idea.

We found out later that the Alzheimer's Society can be a great source of help – we were never signposted there.

## You can get stuff

It was only when I started taking dad to the Veteran's Coffee Mornings that I became aware of Attendance Allowance. This is a benefit available for over 65-year-olds. There are two rates available according to the help and assistance you needed. In the early days dad qualified for the lower rate which offset a little of the carers bills whilst at home. As his condition deteriorated and it was confirmed he needed round the clock care in the care home we could apply for the higher rate. It was a job to complete the form initially though as dad was trying to hide how bad he really was and maybe with an element of pride in the mix, so he was answering questions on the form with a level of untruth, saying how well he could cope on his own. For under 65 year olds, there is something called Personal Independence Payments which is one of the main disability benefits in the UK.

There's also a team in a lot of councils that deal with assisted living devices. We were able to get dad's house assessed and they put measures in place to make his house as safe as it could be. This included grab rails and bath stools in the bathroom, new handrails down the stairs and a step outside the back door. They also sorted us out with the alarm clock that you can record voice reminders into, key fobs that whistle should you lose them, a big dementia friendly clock calendar plus the big button phone that can call someone with just one touch of a button.

Maybe the memory clinic could have signposted us to all the things available; not just the physical aids and the benefits you might qualify for, but the social things too. The Veteran's coffee morning for example. It seemed we found all these things purely by chance.

We heard that if someone goes straight from their own home into a care home, they can claim back twelve weeks of fees. Again, we were completely unaware of this and even if it were true, we would have missed the deadline to claim.

Maybe the care home could have advised?

**Lasting Power of Attorney**

Seriously, without this we would have been scuppered. By having dad sign over his Lasting Power of Attorney to my sister and I – both for finances and health and wellbeing – enabled us to step into his shoes and make decisions on his behalf. This meant we could take over his finances and pay his bills. It meant that we could decide to move him in to the home and keep his bank accounts on track.

Without this in place we would have had no authority, and the nightmare that was the process would have been a hundred times worse.

A Power of Attorney is a legal document drawn up by a solicitor. A person has to be of sound mind to agree to it and with dad's Alzheimer's being a gradual deterioration, there was a point where we wouldn't possibly have been granted it. He would have been too far gone.

## And finally

If you are still here, I thank you for sticking with me on this roller coaster of a journey, and if you are on or have been on a similar one that some of our story rings true with you. You will know that Alzheimer's is a cruel illness that systematically strips away the very substance and foundation of the person it affects. And there is nothing you can do about it except step into their world and deal with it. You always have to remember that it's not the person being difficult, or stubborn or acting out of character. It's the illness making them frightened and confused.

I'll leave you with this poem that my brother read out at dad's funeral.


*Now the Lord of the Realm has glorified the Charge of the Light Brigade,*

*And the thin red line of the Infantry, when will their glory fade?*

*There are robust rhymes on the British Tar and classics on Musketeers,*

*But I shall sing, till your eardrums ring, of the Muddy Old Engineers.*


*Now it's all very fair to fly through the air, or humour a heavy gun,*

*Or ride in tanks through the broken ranks of the crushed and shattered Hun.*

*And its nice to think when the U-Boats sink of the glory that outlives the years,*

*But whoever heard a haunting word for the Muddy Old Engineers?*


*Now you musn't feel, when you read this spiel, that the sapper is a jealous knave,*

*That he joined the ranks for a vote of thanks in search of a hero's grave*

*No your mechanised cavalry's' quite alright and your Tommy has drained few peers,*

*But where in hell would the lot of them be, if it weren't for the Engineers,*

*Oh they look like tramps but they build your camps and sometimes lead the advance,*

*And they sweat red blood to bridge the flood to give you a fighting chance*

*Who stays behind when its getting hot, to blow up the roads in the rear?*

*Just tell your wife she owes your life to some Muddy Old Engineer,*

*Some dusty, crusty, croaking, joking Muddy Old Engineer.*

*No fancy crest is pinned to their chest, if you read what their cap badge says,*

*Why 'Honi Soit Qui Mal Y Pense' is a queersome sort of praise,*

*But their modest claim to immortal fame has probably reached your ears,*

*The first to arrive, the last to leave, the Muddy Old Engineers,*

*The sweating, go getting, uproarious, glorious Muddy Old Engineers.*


*Rudyard Kipling*

Peter McCabe, Bell, George Hoult

## Acknowledgements

Book cover design – Penny Johnson

I'd also like to thank all my friends and family who took the time to proofread this book and add in their takes on the parts that I wasn't actually there for so I could include it accurately.

Thank you all for your amazing, honest feedback that helped me tweak the book to its current state.

Writing down events as they happened really helped shape the book and reading back there were details that I'd even forgotten about, Things we laughed off at the time, but looking back were truly horrendous. Because the decline is slow and subtle you can't put your finger on when things change – but they do.

And writing this has been so therapeutic as dad's legacy and memory live on between these pages.

Dedicated to my one in a million, absolutely awesome dad.

Love you forever xx

Printed in Great Britain
by Amazon